Working in America

Working in America
A Blueprint for the New Labor Market

Paul Osterman
Thomas A. Kochan
Richard Locke
Michael J. Piore

The MIT Press
Cambridge, Massachusetts
London, England

Set in Sabon by The MIT Press.
Printed and bound in the United States of America.

Library of Congress Cataloging-in-Publication Data

Working in America : labor market policies for the new century / Paul Osterman . . . [et al.]
p. cm.
Includes bibliographical references and index.
ISBN 0-262-15105-7 (hc. : alk. paper)
1. Labor market—United States—History—20th century.
2. Manpower policy—United States. I. Osterman, Paul.
HD5724 .W64185 2001
331.12'0973—dc21   2001032619

Contents

Preface

In this book we present the results of nearly 3 years of sustained deliberation concerning the evolution of jobs and the job market in the United States. This effort received its impetus from two worries. First, despite the impressive and sustained expansion of the 1990s, there remain aspects of the American labor market that we find deeply troubling. These include the persistence of a large low-wage labor market, the growth of earnings inequality, the difficulty employees have in obtaining voice in the workplace, and the challenges some firms face in obtaining the flexibility they need to operate in an increasingly competitive market. Perhaps even more troubling was, and is, the absence of a sustained and serious national debate about these concerns. In part, we felt, this was due to the fact that the remaining challenges were being lost in the celebration of prosperity. In part, we felt, it was due to a political stalemate between different sides in some of the debates. Most troubling, we felt, it was due to the absence of a coherent intellectual framework for thinking about and understanding what was new in the American job market and what were the implications of the changed situation for public policy.

Happily, our concerns were shared by program officers at the Ford Foundation and the Rockefeller Foundation, and with their support we launched the Task Force on Reconstructing America's Labor Market Institutions. Our goal was not simply to go off and write a report. Rather, it was to involve a broad range of people in discussing these issues. To that end, we organized 17 workshops, which were attended by 259 people. The topics of these workshops ranged from the evolution of the labor market in the Silicon Valley to the role of unions in the governance of old smokestack industries. These workshops produced rich discussions. We commissioned working papers from experts on many of the relevant topics, many of which are cited in the notes.

A core group of individuals participated in most of the discussions. We called that group the Task Force. Its members, along with all the others who attended the workshops, are listed in the appendixes. As should be apparent, we were able to attract a remarkably able group of people.

The issues we addressed are so controversial that it would not be realistic to expect agreement on all of them from a group of individuals as committed and experienced as those we enlisted. The arguments we present in this volume are ours and ours alone. However, this is a far better document than we could have produced without the participation of so many talented people.

We hope that the ideas we lay out here will be the first step in a broad national dialogue on these issues. We look forward to the debates that are sure to follow.

Acknowledgements

The project upon which this book is based was supported by generous grants from the Ford Foundation and the Rockefeller Foundation. We are grateful to those foundations and to our project officers, Lance Lindblom, Mara Manus, and Katherine McFate, for their support and encouragement.

This book is much stronger as a result of the participation of the hundreds of participants in the Task Force meetings. The core members of the Task Force attended several meetings aimed at improving earlier drafts of the manuscript. We thank all of them for their contributions. A substantial number of colleagues and friends offered written and verbal comments on an earlier draft. We also want to take special note of the insights provided to us by our colleague Robert McKersie.

Several graduate students played important roles in the project. Susan Eaton and Janice Fine helped us think through many of the issues we address in the book. They pressed us in a number of ways to improve our arguments, and we learned a great deal from them. They also generously allowed us to draw upon their research. Forrest Briscoe edited the manuscript and improved it in many ways.

Susan Cass managed the meetings and the preparation of the manuscript in outstanding fashion. Maria Iannozzi provided excellent editorial advice and also did a superb job of producing *Blueprint,* the newsletter of the project. Karen Boyajian provided superb administrative support.

1

Reframing the Debate

The United States entered the new millennium with a confidence and a sense of optimism fueled by the longest economic expansion in its history. Acknowledged as the world's leader in trade, in advanced technology, and in popular culture, it is seen as a model of freedom and prosperity which countries around the world are seeking to emulate, and it is the primary destination of those looking to better their lives through emigration. However, at the same time that the United States has experienced so much prosperity, it has also witnessed the perseverance of income inequality and social dislocation. With the decline of union representation, employees have lost their voice in the workplace. Even during the recent boom, insecurity persisted as layoffs continued. The bottom has fallen out for individuals at the low end of the labor market, leaving too many hard-working Americans frustrated by their inability to earn a living wage. Others are getting by only because they are putting more hours into paid work, which leaves them stretched and stressed as they try to meet family and community obligations. Even among the groups of employees that have benefited most from the upturn in the economy, reports of stress, overwork, job insecurity, and difficulty balancing the dual obligations of work and family are common.

The same good news–bad news paradox applies to other actors in the labor market. Although American industry has prospered in recent years, many firms are finding it increasingly difficult to carry out the functions society expects and in some cases obliges them to perform with respect to steady employment and employee benefits. Indeed, just as the premiums on flexibility, adaptability, and responsiveness to customers and shareholders have increased in recent years, so have employees' expectations of their workplaces. Moreover, in many firms today, particularly those competing in the "new economy," intellectual capital is becoming a critical asset and is challenging traditional employment practices, structures, and in some cases even governance arrangements.

Government has much to be proud of, as is attested by its success in nurturing the long expansion of the 1990s. But with respect to labor and employment policy, government has been caught in a political gridlock for more than 20 years. After incrementally expanding the range of labor-market and workplace regulations between 1960 and 1980, government began to withdraw as an active player in the labor market. This was a response to increased fiscal pressures, but it was also a response to the shift in the political climate that emphasized market mechanisms rather than command-and-control regulations as the most efficient way of dealing with social issues. Yet government regulations of the workplace were not removed from the books. Instead, as budgets for enforcement were reduced and claims by employees grew, enforcement bottlenecks and case backlogs rose at alarming rates. The ideological divide between business and labor—two groups that have historically dominated debates about labor and employment policy—has widened, and policy makers now find that they have little or no room for movement on these issues.

We lack a generally accepted intellectual and policy framework for thinking about the two faces of the current labor market. One view equates economic welfare with social welfare. It sees the competitive-market model as a template for the organization of all productive activity. On this view, economic activity should be organized and directed by independent private decision makers and should be coordinated by prices and wages set in a competitive market. Any institutional restraints on private decisions or on price and wage movements are viewed as interfering with this process and as inherently detrimental to economic and social welfare. This view has driven many structural reforms in the United States (and, with US leadership, in a number of other countries). Deregulation of telecommunication, of airlines, of trucking, and of financial markets has been conceived in these terms. So too has the movement to lower the barriers to trade among countries and to foster international competition. In the labor market, this view has been the major force behind the weakening of protection for labor organizations, the decline of the minimum wage, and the erosion of the unemployment-insurance system. But reforms conceived under the market model have been limited by an institutional perspective, particularly in the labor market.

The institutional perspective recognizes a set of moral values, which individuals seek to realize through work. These values are distinct from economic efficiency and are not necessarily promoted by the market. They include equity and due process in the management of the workplace, equal employment opportunity, work as a creative and dignifying activity, and the right of workers to a voice in the organization and governance of the workplace. An institutional perspective understands the economy as embedded in the social structure and as depending on that structure for its capacity to operate effectively. It sees a need for the active cooperation of workers in the work process, and it emphasizes the difficulty of achieving that cooperation if the non-market values are not respected. And, as the name implies, it recognizes the importance of institutions and the role they play in creating a framework in which a market operates, in mediating the relationship between the economy and society, and in reconciling economic efficiency with other social goals.

We share the institutional perspective if it is understood in these terms. But we seek to go beyond this debate. It is not wise to focus too strongly on the current macroeconomic situation. The better course is to understand how the structure of the economy and that of the labor market have changed and how we should respond to these changes. That is, we emphasize long-term developments rather than current statistics, no matter how impressive or discouraging the current statistics may appear.

By focusing on deeper changes, we attempt to break through the impasse that has arisen. We accept the proposition that the market alone is not sufficient to govern the economy in an efficient or an equitable manner, and we take this as our starting point. But we also recognize that some of the policies and institutions that limited and supplemented the market in the postwar period are no longer consistent with the realities of economic and social life. And because they are not consistent with reality, they are not conducive to the values they were originally designed to achieve. We seek to identify an alternative set of policies and institutions that, in the contemporary environment, will foster the underlying values that the old policies and institutions were originally designed to foster.

The basic argument, briefly stated, is as follows: The current institutional structure housing the labor market and governing work is an outgrowth of New Deal social legislation as it was shaped by court interpretation, legislative amendment, and practice in the course of World War II and the first three postwar decades. The structure was built around three principal organizational actors: the federal government, the corporate employer, and the industrial trade unions. The government set the minimal terms and conditions of employment at the bottom of the labor market. Elsewhere, its role was limited to the creation and enforcement of a set of procedural standards. The substantive terms and conditions of employment were expected to be set through a combination of market forces and through collective bargaining between unions and employers conducted within that procedural framework.

In the 1960s, a second wave of direct social regulation of substantive employment conditions began. Arising initially out of the civil rights movement and the social unrest of that era, the new regulations focused on protecting minorities (and later women, older workers, and other groups) against historic patterns of discrimination. In the 1970s and the 1980s, other regulations were added, covering a range of employment conditions including safety and health, pension funding and administration, mass layoffs and plant closings, and family and medical leave. These regulations were enacted separately and were never integrated with one another or with the New Deal approach to setting minimum standards and encouraging collective bargaining beyond the minimums. As a result, we now have a complex and confusing mix of different avenues of enforcement of workplace rights available to different groups and different remedies available under different statutes.

The policies that emerged from the New Deal and postwar periods were built around a set of assumptions so fundamental that they were hardly even recognized explicitly when introduced. Many of those assumptions, however, have been called into question by the subsequent evolution of the economy and society. The result is a basic mismatch between the institutional structure and the reality of today's world of work.[1] We are concerned in this volume primarily with updating the institutional structures to match the new reality.

The Old Assumptions

Underlying the old system (but undermined by recent changes in the economy and society) were five assumptions.

The first assumption was that the economy of the United States is relatively self-contained and immune from foreign competition and capable of sustaining standardized wages and working conditions across an industry, or even throughout the economy, without handicapping its ability to survive competitively. Indeed, the system was conceived against the backdrop of the Great Depression at a time when the lack of such standards was thought to be responsible for the inability of the economy to sustain a recovery.

Second, the postwar institutional structures were implicitly built around a sharp distinction between the economy and the household. The household was represented in the labor market by a dominant male wage earner or "breadwinner," whose income and benefits were the primary support of the family. Other family members (women, young people) might work for certain periods of time, but their primary commitment was assumed to be to other roles (as homemakers, or as students). Their work was secondary to those commitments, and their income was incidental to the support of the household.

Third, the employment of the head of a household was seen as full-time, long-term, and relatively stable. It was full-time in the sense that the job occupied the entire work week; it was long-term in the sense that most individuals worked for the same enterprise for much if not all of their working lives. Frequent job changing was thought to be characteristic only of young workers searching for their niche, and after a relatively short time they were expected to settle into "permanent" employment and develop careers. Employment was seen as relatively stable in that, with the exception of some periodic downturns of the business cycle that required short-term layoffs (usually only of blue-collar workers), employment was predictable, almost guaranteed.

Linked to the second assumption was a corollary point about where people worked. With the exception of special cases (e.g., the construction trades and parts of the entertainment industry), the traditional assumptions envisioned the typical workplace as a large (often an industrial) firm. Although in reality workers have always been distributed across large and small employers, large enterprises were perceived to be on the vanguard of technology and work practices. Thus, what they did in these areas was seen as progressive and thus as worthy of emulation, even if it did not appear to fit smaller firms.

The temporal and the organizational continuity of employment were underwritten by the fourth assumption: that the corporation was a stable sovereign organization with well-understood boundaries, clearly defined internal roles, and predictable relationships with the external environment. Within the firm, employees were assumed to be grouped into two classes: managers and supervisors ("exempt" employees) and non-managerial workers ("non-exempt" employees). With these labels came different legal rights, obligations, status, and assumed loyalties or commitments to the firm or to one's work group and/or union.

The final assumption concerned the exchange, or implicit social contract, that society came to expect in employment relationships. We use the term "social contract" here simply to capture the expectations and obligations that workers, employers, and society as a whole have for work and employment relationships. The social contract that evolved out of the New Deal and the postwar era generally included the expectation that wages and earnings would rise in tandem with increasing productivity and prosperity. Thus, the fortunes of employers and their workers were intimately linked. Hard work, good performance, and loyalty would be rewarded by employment security, fair treatment, and "good" benefits. Increased tenure with a firm usually provided employees with a kind of "property right" in regard to their job—a right that allowed them to enjoy employment and income security, plan their futures, and prepare for retirement.

The Changing World of Work

Recent changes in the world of work have undermined all these assumptions. In so doing, they have eroded the foundations of the labor market's institutions. The American economy is no longer relatively self-contained and independent; it is embedded in the global economy, and American industry now operates under the constant pressure of foreign competition. The participation rate of women in the labor force has increased enormously, and their role in the household has changed correspondingly. A woman is now more likely to be the head of a household and the sole support of a family. But women also work more frequently and much more steadily even in husband-and-wife families. Their incomes have become essential components of family earnings, and their work is no longer secondary to other roles and responsibilities. Furthermore, many first- and second-generation immigrants have entered the work force. Although some of these immigrant workers have succeeded as entrepreneurs in the new economy,[2] many others have low-end service-sector jobs and hence struggle with low wages, poor or non-existent benefits, and often insecure labor conditions.

The forms of work have also become more varied. Many individuals no longer expect to play out the major portion of their work lives attached to a single employer. Companies have become much more willing to lay off workers, not only (as they always did) in response to business downturns but even in periods of prosperity as shifts in technology and markets change the mix of labor requirements, or in response to pressures from financial markets to increase returns on capital. Workers, in turn, increasingly see the need to move across enterprises to expand their skill base and maintain information networks in the course of their careers. Alternative forms of work and alternative employment relationships have developed through temporary help agencies and independent contracting.

In addition, the corporate enterprise as a well-defined, stable, and enduring organization to which long-term employment rights could be attached is simply disappearing. The boundaries of the firm are being blurred by cross-company work teams, strategic alliances, and subcontracting, and the firm itself is continually being redefined through mergers, acquisitions, and divestitures.

What all this adds up to is that the old social contract, which rested on the expectation that loyalty and good performance would be exchanged for increasing income and employment security, has been broken. The result of these changes is a fundamental mismatch between labor institutions and the deployment of the work force.

There is also a mismatch between individuals' commitments to the labor market and their responsibilities to their families. Opportunities for alternative forms of child or elder care and flexibility in hours or career paths have not kept pace with the increasing labor-force participation of women and the vacuum that this has left in the household. Women (and often men) are increasingly torn between their needs for income and the pressures of their careers and the demands of their children and their aging parents. Also mismatched are the structures of social insurance, job security, family benefits, and career advancement. Each of these is predicated on the head of the household's long-term attachment to an enduring enterprise.

Collective bargaining and its associated labor-management institutions still serve some employees and employers well, particularly where the parties have adapted it to address the changing nature of work and the strategic challenges posed by changing technologies and markets. But collective bargaining's coverage has shrunk to below 10 percent of the private-sector labor force, and access to it is so difficult and fraught with conflict, delays, and risks of job loss that few employees see it as a realistic alternative and few employers are disciplined by the threat of their employees' organizing.

Public policy has been undermined by these mismatches in a variety of ways. We lack strong institutions for linking together a series of short-term work opportunities into a continuous stream of employment and income, now that this function is no longer performed within large enterprises to which workers are permanently attached. We lack institutional guidance for workers negotiating their careers through a sequence of skills developed by moving across the borders of different firms. Coverage by unemployment insurance (originally conceived as an income replacement for workers on temporary layoffs) has declined while the risk of permanent job loss has increased.

It is time to update our policies and institutions to catch up with these changes in the nature of work, in the work force, and in the economy.

The Principles for Labor-Market Institutions

Before we turn to a discussion of policy and institutional re-engineering, let us clarify the values (or what we prefer to call the moral foundations) that we believe should underlie the future labor-market policies and institutions of the United States.

We believe it is time to revisit and recommit to the core values regarding the role of work and its place in society that are embedded in American culture. From the early days of the republic, Americans valued work as a source of dignity and self-fulfillment and put a high premium on freedom of expression and equality of opportunity to achieve individual aspirations and full potential at work. Our vision of the "good society," one that promotes both efficiency and justice, builds on these assumptions.

One of the goals is, of course, economic efficiency. This is sometimes made the predominant goal, and an argument can be made that the labor market should be evaluated in the terms of economic efficiency alone. An efficient system would generate the highest income for workers and the lowest prices for consumers, and workers could then use that income to pursue non-monetary goals outside the workplace, collectively or individually, in their private and civic lives. But workers spend so much time in the workplace that work should not be treated as merely an economic exchange. In fact, because work is typically a social activity, efficiency depends on the quality of the social structures in which it is embedded. Thus, an employment system must be judged on its ability to find and maintain a balance between efficiency and a series of other goals.

In our Task Force meetings,[3] we constantly returned to the point that the rhetoric and (to an extent) the practices of the job market have lost their moral grounding. What values reflecting historic values and cultural traditions should we reassert and recommit ourselves to as we update the policies and institutions governing work? We suggest the following for starters:

Work as a source of dignity   Work is expected to serve society by providing valued goods and services in an efficient manner. But workers should not be treated merely as commodities. All productive work that improves others' welfare, paid or not, should be accorded respect. Work should be encouraged not only because it is good for the economy but also because it is a manifestation of service to the community for the common good.

A living wage   Wages, salaries, and benefits should be sufficient to permit families and individuals to live with dignity and to participate fully in society.

Diversity and equality of opportunity   One of the greatest assets of the United States is a diverse population. This diversity should be embraced, not "managed," and all workers, regardless of their origins, must enjoy the same opportunities to develop skills and to gain access to the jobs of their choice.

Solidarity or social cohesion   We should focus on achieving the common good for all workers, not just material gain for the individual. A society is only as strong as the solidarity manifest within it. Growing disparities in the incomes and life chances of different members of our society weaken our collective strength and cohesiveness and challenge our sense of fairness. We should take a proactive approach to addressing the needs of the most marginalized workers.

Voice and participation   The basic right to freedom of association provides unambiguous support for the right of workers to join unions. We view unions as a positive social and economic institution that helps give workers a voice in regard to their working conditions and a means of achieving their goals at work. But unions are not the only institutions that provide workers with a collective voice. Community and identity groups also play this role in certain contexts. We believe that unions and these other organizations are crucial to enhancing workers' dignity, advancing their interests, and promoting fairness at work.

As we debate policy ideas, we should constantly test them against these values. Obviously the above list does not provide a simple test, and it is equally obvious difficult tradeoffs will have to be made. However, American society has operated in a moral vacuum for too long, perhaps mesmerized by the idea that impersonal market forces would produce efficient and equitable results. We want to move beyond that stance by explicitly recognizing the role of moral choices in the labor market and asking how we can achieve these values in ways consistent with the trends and realities of the market economy as we experience it today.

Learning from Local Experiments

In addition to the values presented above, we believe in what might be termed the principle of subsidiarity: that those closest to the problem possess the best information about the problem and the best idea of how to proceed toward a solution. This view fits well with current circumstances, and a great deal of exciting local experimentation is underway. Indeed, the present moment resembles the early twentieth century in many ways. There was a sense then, as there is now, that the inherited institutions and organizational structures were no longer appropriate for the technological and economic environment. There was widespread experimentation with new business strategies and structures, new forms of worker organization, and different patterns of government control, regulation, and social insurance. The effort to forge new structures more appropriate for an industrial economy moved to the national level with the Great Depression and the New Deal. The main elements of the system that emerged in the 1930s and was consolidated in the early postwar period were distilled from this earlier experience of decentralized experimentation.

The parallels between that earlier period and our own led us to look for comparable experimentation in local responses today. We did indeed find a very wide array of responses at the community level, many creative and innovative. They were present in businesses, among local and national unions, and in non-profit, non-governmental organizations that did not fit easily into any of the existing institutional categories. These local efforts expose the sterility of the national-level debate about labor institutions. This volume is grounded in these local efforts and is driven in no small measure by our excitement at their range and quality.

But if the *inspiration* for looking to local experimentation derives from the process through which new institutional structures emerged in the early part of the twentieth century, the results of our survey of recent local innovations are very different. What finally emerged from the earlier period was a clear set of dominant institutions. Even the centrality of the federal government, which actually developed only in the New Deal, reflected the lessons learned about the limits of the programs that state and local governments had experimented with before. The hallmark of the present period is the enormous variety of particular circumstances in which local communities find themselves and of the organizations and institutions that are emerging in response. The first task in constructing a new set of policies and institutions appears to be to recognize and accommodate that variety. Thus, an important goal of this volume is to understand the changing roles and responsibilities of business, unions, and government, to highlight the growing importance of new actors, and to suggest how to capitalize on existing diversity and experimentation. A brief preview of how we see these actors and their relationships changing follows.

Employers

The New Deal system of labor relations and employment relations envisioned employers as the institution through which most of the labor market's important functions and services would be funded and delivered. Individual firms were given responsibilities for funding unemployment insurance, social security, private pensions, health insurance, vacation and leave policies, training, and other terms and conditions of employment and/or for negotiating the funding of these provisions with unions. The case studies we present in chapter 3 suggest that a number of large corporations continue to play a role very similar to the role that was assumed in the New Deal system. They offer their workers a high degree of job security and a range of employment benefits that bind them to the enterprise. And they are actively experimenting with new benefits that seek to align work requirements with the social structure outside the workplace, much as businesses in the 1920s and in the immediate postwar period pioneered new pension and medical benefits. Moreover, those firms that innovate in one area tend to innovate in several—in the vernacular of modern day human-resources management, they "bundle" their practices to fit their strategies, values, and needs of hard-to-replace workers. For example, firms that adopt what are called "high-performance work practices" are also more likely to adopt flexible policies aimed at helping employees balance work and family responsibilities. Even these leading employers, however, have abandoned the business model that underlay the old system. The scope and the structure of the business are subject to continual financial calculation. Employment and the terms and conditions on which it is offered are contingent on markets and technologies that are likely to change. The organization is, in principle, focused on its core competencies; work that is not directly related to these competencies is subcontracted. The employment conditions a company offers, even though they resemble those of the postwar era, are extended to a much smaller group of people relative to those whose economic welfare is ultimately linked to the company's activities, and the size and the shape of the corporation are open to continuous revision through merger, acquisition, divestiture, and subcontracting.

At the other extreme on the spectrum of employment are workers who essentially operate as independent contractors, moving from employer to employer with no stability or employment security. A substantial majority of these individuals prefer this arrangement because it allows them to earn more in the short run and to learn by taking on new and challenging assignments that expand their professional networks. These mobile professionals therefore need labor-market institutions that foster mobility, provide access to information on emerging technologies and job opportunities, and help them to afford health insurance and to invest an adequate portion of their earnings for the long term and/or for their eventual retirement.

In between the extremes of the independent contractors and stable large firms are a wide range of temporary-help services and subcontracting firms that provide an increasing array of specialized services heretofore performed inside larger integrated enterprises. Some of these provide portals to permanent employment (a new form of recruitment); others provide flexibility for individuals who want part-time or short-term jobs while they attend to personal, family, or educational tasks. But some are only second-best options for workers unable to find jobs that provide more security, higher pay, and access to benefits. Dealing with "contingent" employers and employees is perhaps one of the biggest challenges facing public policy today.

Then there are the many interesting new organizations that are arising from the information- or Internet-based economy. These are taking on a variety of forms and have yet to settle into a stable pattern. Early evidence on these firms suggests that human resources are especially important to their success or failure.[4] This is not surprising, since intellectual capital is an asset of many of these entrepreneurial organizations (and a major asset of some). These emerging organizations may tell us a great deal about how employment relationships will be shaped in the future, since their employment practices, like those of their predecessors, will likely make a lasting imprint on employment relations. Fostering positive models now might, therefore, pay long-term dividends for the economy and the work force.

We must also keep in mind that the work force is distributed across a relatively small number of large employers and a very large number of small ones. For example, of the approximately 6 million establishments in the United States, nearly 92 percent employ fewer than 50 workers. These small firms employ 43 percent of the work force and are a significant factor in any discussion of employment policy.

In view of the variety of organizational forms now found in the economy and the changed business models under which firms now operate, society must be careful not to attempt to load all responsibilities for delivering labor-market functions and services back onto individual firms or single employment relationships. In a world where the boundaries of firms are unstable and where (because of mobility) which employees are covered by firm-specific policies and which employees are not changes frequently, we can no longer expect individual firms to accept responsibility for solving all labor-market problems. But this does not mean that we should absolve individual firms of the responsibility to be good employers or responsible citizens of their communities. If individual firms acting alone can no longer carry out the range of employment functions expected of them in the past, we must encourage them to work in collaboration with labor-market institutions and community organizations.

Unions and Professional Associations

When we think of labor-market institutions other than firms, the institutions that come most readily to mind are unions. And in the United States, when we think of unions we immediately think of collective bargaining. Yet union membership has been declining in the United States for more than 40 years, and unions now represent less than 10 percent of the private-sector labor force— about the same percentage as just before the surge in union membership at the beginning of the New Deal. We see this as a serious problem for American society.

We believe strongly and firmly, as do the vast majority of Americans, that unions have an important and necessary role to play in American society. As a result, in this volume we examine what unions are doing to reinvent themselves and to create what one of our Task Force members calls "next-generation unions." We offer ideas for how the roles of unions, professional associations, and other organizations that give employees a voice might change in the future. Moreover, though we also believe very strongly in the value of collective bargaining as an instrument by which unions contribute to shared prosperity, we foresee the unions of the future seeking to promote mobility of workers, to provide individual labor-market services and benefits to members, to support direct employee voice on the job, to create and co-direct labor-management partnerships at the firm, community, and industry levels, and to work with other groups to promote employees' interests and welfare.

Similar to the case with employers, increased diversity is apparent in emergent union structures. The history of union organization in the United States is marked by a clear succession in the dominant mode of organization as the economy evolved from its agrarian roots in the nineteenth century into a dominant industrial power in the twentieth. The evolution, moreover, followed a clear succession of forms, beginning with friendly societies and cooperatives in the early nineteenth century through the craft unions that emerged in the later part of that century to the mass industrial unions that emerged in the Great Depression and came to dominate the labor movement in the immediate postwar period.

Our case studies did indeed uncover new organizational forms, but no single form appears to be emerging as dominant. In some industries, mass industrial unions continue to be dominant and continue to bargain with employers in much the same way they did throughout the postwar period. But craft unions and professional associations, which were largely eclipsed by the emergence of industrial unionism in the 1930s, have exhibited a renewed vitality and are experimenting with a variety of techniques for organizing and representation.

In many ways, these occupation-centered organizations are better matched to a labor market in which individuals are not attached to a single employer and therefore need not move across employers in order to maintain both employment and skill development. At the same time, some of these professional associations have begun to take on more of the functions typically associated with more traditional craft and industrial unions. The organization of medical doctors, for example, was driven in part by the consolidation of the health industry into large, bureaucratic organizations very similar to what industrial workers in an earlier era encountered in manufacturing. But doctors (and other medical professionals) are organizing around their occupational identities and are fighting to maintain a degree of professional autonomy in a manner similar to that which craft unions achieve for their members. In the low-wage labor market, however, worker organizations are trying to form across craft and industrial lines and to preserve continuity of employment for individuals who have none of the traditional attachments at all except a need to work continuously in a particular geographic location.

One unresolved problem all these unions face is difficulty in recruiting and retaining members as individuals change employers and occupations. A new approach is needed that will make it easier for individuals to join, remain attached to, and be represented and served by a union or an association. This new approach will have to match the nature of today's work force and economy. (We will suggest what we call a networked model of unionism.)

Community Groups and Labor-Market Intermediaries

The growing importance of new community-level actors in the labor market is dramatic and exciting. Many of these groups work in tandem or in coalition with unions or were first supported by unions, and therefore they too can be viewed as complements to traditional unions. Some tend to be grounded in ethnic or religious communities, or in other communities of interest (such as the Industrial Areas Foundation network). Others are organized around specific identities, such as profession, gender, or sexual orientation. We also see a growing role for a broad range of labor-market intermediaries, some of which (e.g., temporary help agencies) are complements to firms, some of which (e.g., the National Urban League) seek to address the labor-market needs of specific categories of workers, and some of which (e.g., the Federal Mediation and Conciliation Service, the Regional Employment Boards, and the growing network of work/family intermediaries) mediate between firms and workers. These institutions play several important roles. In some instances they are vehicles for employee voice and advocacy. They are also often effective labor-market intermediaries. We will argue that the increase in job turnover and mobility has created the potential for a stronger role for intermediaries, and that institutions which play this role can leverage this function into effective labor-market power on behalf of employees. Some provide training, and that function is likely to become more important as requirements for lifelong learning increase. Others (such as family and work nonprofit and for-profit organizations that serve mostly professional workers) work more directly with or for firms. On an international scale, a variety of nongovernmental organizations are emerging that seek to monitor and upgrade labor standards in developing countries. These innovations fall squarely in the American tradition of letting local experimentation be the basis for subsequent national policy making. It will be important to understand the strengths and limits of these institutions, to build up their capacities, and to apply their lessons to national policy making.

Government

Diversity in the economy and in the work force calls for new roles for various levels of government. We propose a new role for government as a complement to private firms and institutions—a role that facilitates change and innovation, regulates with an eye toward greater flexibility, and is grounded in an updated set of labor and employment policies. And we see the functions of government more broadly shared across the federal, state, local, and transnational levels, in contrast to the position of dominance for the federal government that was built into the New Deal policies.

Like the other actors, government policy must be driven by clear values and by strategies for achieving the desired outcomes in the labor market. These strategies must be derived from a clear and up-to-date understanding of how workers and employers interact and of what they need to prosper in the present-day economy. Such a strategic vision, and the leadership required to implement it, have been sorely lacking in government policy and its administration. However, in urging a more proactive, more strategic approach by government, we must be cognizant of the deep-seated fear of "too much government" that is embedded in the American culture.

Government policy must also recognize the diversity of the economy and of employment relationships, and it must move beyond a singular command-and-control enforcement mode and seek ways to draw on the potential of private institutions—individual companies, unions, dispute-resolution institutions, and community-based organizations—to assist and complement the role of traditional enforcement regimes. Instead of starting from the premise that all employment relationships should be regulated in the same way, we should work from the premise that all employment relationships should be held accountable for achieving the goals or moral foundations we laid out at the beginning of this chapter. *How* these goals are achieved might well differ between employers that have highly sophisticated and advanced human-resources and labor-management policies and that work in collaborative fashion with employee organizations and/or cross-cutting labor-market institutions and employers that have more traditional or less well-developed workplace policies and practices or those that do not respect workers' basic rights or are unwilling to work with external institutions.

Building Bridges and Including New Voices

Although we recognize the importance of decentralized local experiments and the importance of reconfiguring the roles of traditional social actors, we acknowledge that if such experiments are to have real impact they will have to be ratified, supported, and "scaled up" by national policies. How can that be achieved? We propose two mechanisms.

First, the United States should develop a more inclusive and deliberative policy-making process.[5] As we have suggested throughout this chapter, the process we have in mind would, wherever possible, devolve decision making to the actual actors and/or interests most affected by the policies—the actors who possess the information necessary to shape policy and who are best able to implement or monitor the policies. This would enhance regulatory efficiency and would reduce its rigidity and intrusiveness. In exchange for this quasi-public role in the policy-making process, these organized actors should be representative, should allow the full range of interests to participate in the deliberative processes, should be internally democratic and accountable, and should communicate with other groups. The range of groups and/or actors in this process will have to be much wider than the traditional interest groups; it will have to give voice to viewpoints that already exist (often unheard) in the labor market. Some of these forums may be located within individual firms, but increasingly we see the need for cross-cutting community-level institutions that will engage local employers with community groups, employee organizations, and public officials.

Second, policy reform should be promoted by the construction of cross-class and cross-group coalitions.[6] This will require addressing a variety of "bridging issues"—issues that matter to and thus can mobilize various categories of workers and other groups in society. Work/family issues and issues of training or lifelong learning quickly come to mind. Employees at all levels of the labor market—especially younger workers who are starting a family and older employees who need to care for an ill or aged relative—struggle to balance or integrate the competing claims of work and family, often at great cost to themselves. Individual companies would benefit from greater options in this area, since work/family matters can affect an individual's productivity and a company's ability to recruit and retain skilled workers. Policies likely to alleviate these tensions and to promote greater balance would certainly bring different kinds of employees together; they would also bring different kinds of employers and public authorities together. Improved training arrangements might also create common ground among these labor-market actors. In today's fast-changing economy, the premium on skill and knowledge is at an all-time high. Individual employers complain that they cannot find (let alone retain) employees with the requisite skills. Yet many individual companies hesitate to invest in training for fear that the investment will be wasted when rival firms poach their most valued (and recently trained) employees.

Likewise, individual employees in many different occupations crave greater learning opportunities, since they realize that their career trajectories and their future employability depend on their possession of up-to-date skills. Government policy makers have long struggled with ways of enhancing the availability and quality of training for current and perspective workers. Where government, firms, and unions have managed to come together and experiment with new forms of training, extremely interesting results have emerged.[7]

In short, we believe that a more inclusive process of policy reform can be launched in the United States. This process must be guided by and must balance concerns for economic efficiency, for equality, and for the welfare of the whole society. Government continues to be an important player in this process, participating in the discussions and deliberations, guaranteeing that the conditions and norms of the process are maintained, using fiscal incentives and other means to shape the process, and assisting in the scaling up of promising local experiments. Such a policy-making process is consistent with the approaches advocated by the previous generation of reformers and reflects the consensus principles for democratic decision making and multiparty negotiations common to an increasing number of public policy realms.

Conclusion

The mismatch between the labor-market institutions that we have inherited from the New Deal and the present-day economy has significant consequences when the economy is performing well and labor markets are tight; it will be even more problematic in times when the economy slows down and unemployment rises. Our laws and institutions do not account for the diversity of employers, and this will prove costly to organizations as they struggle to compete in an increasingly difficult environment. Employees do not have the voice they deserve or the assistance and protection they need in a volatile, high-turnover labor market. The ongoing problems in low-income labor markets seem inexcusable in good times and will be deeply troubling in the future.

We believe that the labor-market policies and institutions of the United States must be reconstructed. We also believe that this process is underway in numerous localities as firms, unions, and community groups struggle to invent new ways of doing business. This is the classic manner in which social innovation occurs in the United States. This volume aims to bring these efforts to light, to distill the essential principles which we believe should guide the new labor market, and to lay out the roles that firms, unions, and the federal government should play in this process. There is a great deal of energy and good will to draw upon, and we are optimistic.

2

Tracing the Shifting Labor Market

The labor-market policies and institutions of the New Deal were based on a set of assumptions that work could be classified into discrete categories: exempt versus non-exempt, supervisory versus non-supervisory, full-time family breadwinners versus career employees and part-timers with primary attachments to family or other non-work activities, union versus non-union, and so on. Within these categories, regulations and practices sought to standardize conditions and "take labor out of competition" and thereby to set a common floor for working conditions and lay the foundation for their gradual improvement. Over time, however, the labor market and the nature of work and employment have grown in complexity and variety to the point that the categories have become less useful for guiding policy and practice. This mismatch between the realities of today's labor market and the policy and institutions governing work and labor-market activity is at the core of many of the problems and tensions experienced by workers and employers today.

This chapter summarizes the changes in labor markets that gave rise to the current diversity and complexity and identifies the challenges they raise for the task of updating policies and institutions. We will focus on five major developments:

Changes in who is working Perhaps the most dramatic change in this category has been the increased role of women, evident not only from the rate of participation in the labor force but also from the hours devoted to paid work and the gradual movement of women into traditionally male-dominated jobs and positions of authority. This change has moved work/family issues onto the front burner, yet our labor-market institutions are poorly structured to deal effectively with these concerns. The work force is becoming more diverse on ethnic, racial, and other cultural dimensions too. The United States has historically been a nation of immigrants, and immigration continues to make its work force more diverse. Competing effectively and living and working together harmoniously will increasingly depend on respecting and learning from diversity and on creating institutions suitable for a global marketplace.

Changes in how people work   The rapid spread of new ideas about how to organize work and about how work relates to technology and information, typically under the rubric of "high performance" or that of "knowledge," has brought substantial gains in productivity and quality. However, these ideas also have increased the demand for skilled workers, perhaps exacerbating the growth of inequality, and have undermined traditional distinctions (embodied in labor and employment law) between managers and employees. In addition, the shifting and increasingly unclear boundaries between organizations pose considerable challenges, particularly for unions, as the traditional locus of organization becomes less and less stable. The exploding demand for workers with the technical skills needed to support startups and older firms seeking to compete in the "new" or "Internet" economy is shifting the patterns of compensation and is creating a need for new intermediaries able to match supply to demand in this sector.

Increased flexibility and mobility in the labor market   Firms need to respond to uncertain and changing markets and technologies; therefore, they eschew long-term commitments and slow-to-change institutional contracts. Employees too value flexibility, albeit of a different kind: they value the ability to take advantage of new opportunities and the flexibility needed to meet varying family and work responsibilities. Long-term attachments between workers and firms are weakening. This shows up in a variety of ways, from increased turnover to the growth of contingent work. This development poses substantial challenges for the safety net (health care and pensions), for the effective facilitation of movement through the job market, and for the ability of unions and professional associations to increase their influence in a labor market that looks increasingly unlike the one on which their traditional models are based.

The higher premium for skills and learning   Employees need new and higher skills in order to cope with the changed environment. Although skills are not sufficient (and we argue throughout this volume that new institutional supports must be constructed), they are necessary. Firms too rely heavily on human capital and learning as competitive assets, some of which may be possessed by their employees and some of which may lie elsewhere. The net result of these developments is that the wage premiums attached to education and skills have increased dramatically in the past two decades. As technologies change and as knowledge advances, lifelong learning or continuous investment is needed to keep an individual's skills current.

The shift in the mix of private and public means for improving, expanding, and monitoring labor standards and working conditions   Over the past 40 years, the percentage of workers organized by unions has been declining and government's regulation of labor standards and employment outcomes has been increasing. It was a basic premise of the New Deal labor and employment legislation was that the government would set minimum standards on a limited array of employment conditions and leave to it to market forces and unions to negotiate improvements and expansions on these minimums, but as unions declined society turned to government as a means of addressing workplace problems not taken care of by market forces. Although the rate of expansion in government regulations has slowed considerably since 1980, the task of enforcement has grown for government agencies, the task of compliance has become more difficult for employers, and the task of processing claims has become more difficult and costly for employees.

These changes will now be taken up in more detail.

Changes in Who Is Working

Although diversity has always been a hallmark of American society and its labor force, it is even more so today than ever before, and the nature of diversity is shifting. Approximately 25 percent of the population is now non-white, and this percentage is projected to increase to 35 by 2020 and roughly 50 by the middle years of this century. The immigration that has occurred in the past several decades and the immigration that is likely to occur in the future will add to America's racial and cultural diversity. In the nineteenth century and in the early years of the twentieth century, most immigrants to the United States came from Europe. Now, Asia and Latin America account for the largest numbers of new immigrants.

These well-known trends mask an equally important but less obvious source of diversity in the labor force that produces goods and services for American companies and consumers. In the world's current markets for capital and labor, national boundaries have less meaning. Since different parts of the value chain of a product can move more freely to alternative locations, organizations, and countries, efforts to regulate labor or to create new labor-market institutions must consider the global market for labor as well as the work physically performed within national boundaries. This increases the importance of international labor standards. Such standards have traditionally been viewed as a subset of human rights, and recently the International Labor Organization reaffirmed this view by identifying certain labor standards dealing with child labor, slave labor, discrimination, and freedom to join a union as fundamental human rights.[1] However, labor standards and working conditions are increasingly prominent in policy debates on trade. There are highly divergent views on the role labor standards should play in trade, and we will join this debate directly in chapter 6. For now, it is sufficient to note that any effort to update labor-market policies and institutions must take the growing importance of cross-border trade into account.

Another important shift has been the increased participation of women in the labor market. The central facts are well known. The percentage of women who are working has increased—and this percentage understates the heightened pressure, since it does not take changes in the composition of families into account. The percentage of mothers with children under age 6 who have no spouse has increased. And these women are more likely to be working than in the past—a trend that has been accelerated by welfare reform. (The number of welfare recipients who work has tripled since 1992.)

The increase in hours worked is another change that has increased the pressure on families. Working women are working more hours. From 1969 to 1996 there was a 24 percent increase in hours worked by married women; among single mothers, the increase was 8 percent.[2]

There was an increase of 497 hours of work per year (18 percent) for two-parent families between 1969 and 1996; for single parents the increase was 297 hours (28 percent). All of this increase came from women; the annual hours of work among men remaining flat.[3]

As evidence that these trends have placed considerable pressure on families, consider the following:

• In 1996, 22 percent of households provided informal care to a relative or friend over the age of 50. Of the caregivers, two-thirds worked and three-fourths were women.[4]

• Thirty-eight percent of working women cite child care or elder care as the reason they work non-standard hours.[5]

• Of the 7.3 million Americans who cannot perform daily tasks, more than half are cared for by younger family members who are not their spouses.[6]

The private sector's responses to these developments have been uneven and incomplete. Though concerns about work and family have been given a prominent place in public discussions and in the media, the overwhelming majority of working Americans surveyed report that they have little support in this area. A 1992 survey of a representative sample of private-sector establishments with 50 or more employees found that only 12 percent of employers provided day care or financial assistance for it.[7] A 1997 survey found that 36 percent of employers provided low-cost assistance, such as workshops and help-lines, and 9 percent provided day care at or near the place of employment. What has increased is the number of firms with formal or informal policies allowing flexibility in hours and/or opportunities to work at home. A 1997 survey indicated that 68 percent of large firms offered the former and about 20 percent offered the latter to at least some of their employees.[8]

There are a variety of reasons for believing that a simple expansion of employer-based work/family programs would be an inadequate response. Evidence suggests that, even when policies such as flexible hours are in place, employees are reluctant to take advantage of them because of fears that this will be viewed as evidence of a lack of commitment.[9] Most of the more complete versions of firm-based work/family support have been directed at professional and managerial employees, leaving the majority of lower-paid employees with little help. And, as mobility in the labor market increases, relying on firm-specific benefits becomes more and more problematic.

Thus, in contrast with the 1930s, when it may have been reasonable to envision the prototypical worker as a male blue- or white-collar industrial worker, today there is no single prototype around which to build policies and institutions. Now one must start from the assumption that the work force is diverse.

Changes in How People Work

Another major development in the labor market has been the blurring of boundaries between workers and management. At least since the New Deal, a clear view of how work is organized has been embedded both in law and in policy. On that view, there is a sharp and identifiable divide between the activities of managers and those of workers, the former being responsible for conception and planning and the latter for execution. This view is embodied in American labor law by the exclusion of managers from protection under the National Labor Relations Act and by restrictions on the ability of managers to consult groups of workers on topics that are considered terms and conditions of employment (lest the workers be viewed as constituting a company-dominated union). It is also embodied in a similar distinction between managers and professional employees (who typically are classified as exempt from the overtime provisions and selected other provisions of wage and hour law) and "non-exempt" workers, who presumably are paid on an hourly basis for doing lower-level production or service work. Since the mid 1980s, substantial shifts in the organization of work have undermined these distinctions and thus have cast doubt on the basis of at least some elements of labor-market governance.

One of the most important ways in which American firms responded to competitive challenges in the 1980s and the early 1990s was by adopting what came to be termed "high-performance" or "knowledge-based" work practices. These terms are most commonly applied to blue-collar work, but many of the innovations they embody are equally applicable in other settings. We will discuss the new work practices in more detail in chapter 3. For present purposes, it is sufficient to note that they are now accepted as state-of-the-art principles for work and organization design. Any effort to update policies and institutions governing work must take these work practices into account.

Another important development not anticipated by the New Deal policies and institutions is the increased variation in where and when people work. Innovations in communications technologies are blurring the distinctions between work and home, between work and commuting, and between work and recreation. Consider the difficulty government regulators are having with the concept of work at home. In the 1930s, regulations limiting home work were aimed at eliminating the practice of sending parts of garments to homes to be sewn under unsafe conditions at wages below the minimum. Today, work at home is most likely to be done by means of a computer, a fax or Internet connection, or a cell phone. In view of the ubiquity of these devices, it is nearly impossible to estimate the percentage of people who do part of their jobs at home, much less to design regulations governing such work. Much to its chagrin, the US Occupational Safety and Health Administration realized this recently when (presumably by mistake) it issued a letter advising an employer that it had an obligation to ensure that the physical setting in which home work was being performed conformed to OSHA standards. This directive lasted one day before the Secretary of Labor ordered it rescinded in response to the negative reactions it generated among employers and the general public. No standard regulations can effectively govern the multiplicity of settings in which work is performed today.

The technologies that now offer greater flexibility both to employers and to employees pose challenges to traditional management and supervisory methods, and for employees they increases the reach of work into private settings.[10]

The variation in work hours among individuals and the variation among individuals with respect to project cycles, organizational life cycles, or individual career stages challenge any effort to think through whether and how to update regulations that govern working time. Practices standardized by means of national regulations, or even perhaps by means of standard provisions of collective bargaining agreements or company-written personnel policies, are likely to be viewed as too rigid and as unable to address the varied circumstances encountered at work today. More decentralized and informal institutions or processes that will give workers greater control of their work schedules are needed. Yet solutions still require consensus among, or at least the support of, groups of workers and managers. A simple bilateral "deal" between an individual and his or her supervisor is not likely to be workable or stable, since others either will be directly affected by the "deal" or will perceive it to be inequitable relative to what they see others doing.

Increased Flexibility and Mobility

The press and the popular culture are replete with assertions and anecdotes pointing to the erosion of stable careers. These observations seem to be ratified by nearly daily announcements of layoffs and restructuring, even in a remarkably strong economy. As striking as the stories are, this is a very large economy, and it is prudent to search for broader and more representative evidence of the declining security of careers. One important source of such evidence is the Current Population Survey, which includes data on the distribution of job tenure. Job tenure, which represents the number of years an employee has been with his or her current employer, is an important clue to what is happening to careers. Table 2.1 shows the distribution of tenure for men and women in three age groups.[11] The data show a sharp drop in tenure for men and a mild gain in tenure for women (which is probably related to the increasing commitment of women to the labor market). Overall, tenure has fallen.

Table 2.1
Median years of job tenure. Source: Bureau of Labor Statistics.

Age	Men		Women	
	1983	1998	1983	1998
35–44	7.3	5.5	4.1	4.5
45–54	12.8	9.4	6.3	7.2
55–64	15.3	11.2	9.8	9.6

Perhaps an even more fundamental shift is that in the past several decades a rapidly growing percentage of those in the work force have found themselves working in what has come to be called contingent employment. In the past, temporary work arose either because of seasonality (as when stores hire extra clerks before Christmas) or from the need to fill in for absent employees on a short-term basis. Today the use of contingent workers has become a much more central and intrinsic part of a firm's operations. In 1996, office and clerical jobs accounted for only 30 percent of the revenue of the "staffing industry" (the term preferred by the temporary-help agencies).[12] Some companies use employees of temporary-help agencies to permanently staff significant portions of their operations—especially call-center or customer-service operations.[13] In other instances, firms replace the traditional probationary period by contracting for temporary workers and then selecting some of them for permanent hiring. In these cases, temporary-help agencies perform recruitment and intermediary functions. In yet other instances, temporary workers and permanent employees work side by side, and the employer can easily reduce staffing by cutting back on the temporary portion. (In the last case, of course, there is also the option of gradually shifting a larger fraction of the work to the contingent group.)

The shift in nature of temporary work embodies a re-thinking of a firm's relationship with and its obligations to its work force. Furthermore, the employees who find themselves in temporary jobs are almost certain to be more mobile than "standard" employees and hence will have to deal with the aforementioned challenges faced by a less attached and less secure labor force. In addition, although a considerable fraction of contingent workers are content with their circumstances, for many others these jobs provide less pay and fewer benefits than comparable employees in more regular positions receive.

In 1995, 1997, and 1999 the Current Population Survey asked employed individuals about the nature of their work. Data from that survey are shown in table 2.2. Relative to the entire labor force, the percentage of contingent employees was not great. This is not surprising; even small percentage changes can lead to large absolute numbers in an economy as large as that of the United States and hence can catch people's attention. However, another source of data—the Current Employment Statistics (generated by surveys of establishments, whereas the Current Population Survey is a survey of individuals)—suggests larger numbers. The CES collects data on employment by industry, and one of the industries is Personnel Supply Services, which is basically equivalent to temporary-help agencies. For reasons that are

Table 2.2
Percentage of labor force accounted for by different types of contingent workers. Source: Current Population Survey, 1995, 1997, 1999.

	1995	1997	1999
Independent contractor or freelance	6.7	6.7	6.3
On call	1.6	1.6	1.5
Agency temporaries	1.0	0.9	0.9
Contract workers	0.6	0.5	0.6

not well understood, the CES shows employment levels well above those of the CPS. (The CES data are shown in table 2.3.) Even the CES data show that less than 3 percent of the labor force is employed by temporary-help agencies; however, these data show impressively rapid growth.

In assessing these numbers it is also important to remember that they represent the stock of employees who, at any point in time, are contingent. Because contingent assignments are often short term, it is likely that a larger fraction of employees are contingent at some point in a year. The National Establishment Survey found the median duration of a contingent or temporary job to be 5 months.[14] Hence, depending on whether the same individuals or different individuals move through a series of short-term assignments, the fraction of employees who are contingent at some point of the year may be up to twice as large as the fraction who are contingent at any particular time.

What are the human consequences of the increased mobility in the labor market? The story is mixed, and in many respects the new market offers positive opportunities for many individuals. Economists have long celebrated the virtues of job searching and information gathering in the labor market, particularly for younger workers, and those activities entail high mobility. It seems also clear that in a strong labor market workers with scarce and valuable skills will do well and will often move to employers who are willing to make better offers.

Table 2.3
Employment by personnel-supply services. Source: http://www.bls.gov/cestabs.htm

	Number employed	As percentage of total employment
1979	507,800	0.5
1989	1,454,500	1.3
1999	3,600,000	2.7

Silicon Valley appears in many respects to be the epitome of such a labor market. Mobility appears to be at the heart of the Silicon Valley model. AnnaLee Saxenian reports that "careers in Silicon Valley are rarely defined within the boundaries of a single firm" and that "individuals move frequently between companies—from small to large firms and vice versa, from established companies to startups, and even between industries and sectors—and most report loyalties to a particular team or to advancing technology rather than to an individual company."[15] Gideon Kunda, Steven Barley, and James Evans found that many "high-end" contingent workers in Silicon Valley were well satisfied with their circumstances. Two things they enjoyed were freedom from corporate politics and the opportunity to learn new skills. One contractor reported:

Probably most of the jobs I've had were valuable in a way because the thing I like with consulting is I get to do different things. An I know there's an end to it and I can do another project. I was offered a full-time job; I did consider it, but when I though about it, I realized I would still be doing the same thing. So I opted not to take it.

Another contractor said:

[T]hat is something else I really like about contracting, the wackos out there. You get a chance to see a lot of different technologies, not necessarily new technology. You see all these different applications, different people, different perspectives. Some are great, some are horrible, but it is interesting, it is exciting.[16]

The success of individuals, even in freewheeling Silicon Valley, rests upon (or, in more fashionable language, is embedded in) well-developed social networks. Such networks are precisely what the individuals who are not making it in today's economy lack. This point is illustrated by the following quotation from one of the aforementioned contractors:

Job security is the ability to get a job. Staff people don't have job security: you can be fired whenever the company likes. And they don't have networks. They can't call someone and get a job tomorrow morning.

They think they have job security but it's on paper. People don't realize that real job security is when you have a network of managers and recruiters where you simply call them and say "OK, my contract finished," and they say "Great, I can place you somewhere tomorrow morning." The social reality is, the staff person has no connections to the next job. They don't have social relationships. They're isolated. A contractor has these relationships. That's real job security. That's the real game.[17]

The networks referred to above are informal and may seem to rest on the efforts of individuals. In this sense they might be characterized as part of an individual's human capital. However, Silicon Valley is also home to more formal structures that perform the same function for far more people—for example, the formal ethnic networks and associations in Silicon Valley (the Silicon Valley Indian Professionals Association, the Chinese Software Professional Association, the Monte Jade Science and Technology Association, and so on), which connected people to jobs and to opportunities.[18] Without these networks, tens of thousands of individuals would have done much less well. For example, according to the founder of the Silicon Valley Indian Professionals Association "many Indians didn't see a career path beyond what they were doing," and the association therefore focused on helping individuals design career strategies as well as on conveying technical information regarding the industry.[19]

In short, for many individuals in Silicon Valley mobility is a good thing. It is also the case, however, that for many in Silicon Valley and elsewhere increased job turnover is a dangerous proposition.

Involuntary job loss has considerable consequences. Data from surveys of dislocated workers show that nearly 40 percent of the victims of large-scale layoffs or plant closings suffered earnings losses of 20 percent or more.[20]

The risks of dislocation extend even to young people, whose career prospects one might expect to be resilient. From data gathered by the National Longitudinal Survey of Youth, Cynthia Gustafson concludes that displacement reduces subsequent earnings by 14 percent.[21]

We can get a good sense of the consequences of contingent work by drawing on the Current Population Survey. Perhaps the most basic question is whether people want contingent jobs. The pattern is clear: whereas independent contractors are contented, individuals working for temporary-help agencies or in jobs of limited duration or as on-call workers overwhelmingly would prefer standard employment.[22] A good illustration is the following description of the advantages of temporary work, from an interview conducted in Silicon Valley by Charles Darrah: "It doesn't allow you to work your way up in the company, but it does allow you to work your way up switching companies. I understand a lot of people use temping as a way to find a place they would like to become permanent."[23]

At the same time, temporary work raises difficult issues regarding who in an employment relationship is the responsible employer (i.e., the employer who is legally accountable). There is no consistent definition of the employer across all the federal and state regulations governing employment. This raises issues of cost and complexity for many employers; it also means that individuals may find that they lack employment protection. Consider how one of the "temps" interviewed by Darrah described a sexual-harassment problem:

One thing that is really like a pet peeve is that working as a temp really negates all kind of issues, like discrimination on the job, even sexual harassment because if you raise these issues it runs the possibility of the employer saying, "You know what? We're investigating." And then they'll caucus and they'll say, "It's got nothing to do with the issues that were raised by you, but the assignment is finished and we're going to call you back and we'll meet with you on these issues, and we're going to call you back as soon as there is something coming in and I think that'll probably be another day. Call me or I'll call you.[24]

How does contingent employment affect economic well being? To begin, contingent workers receive lower pay and are more likely to work part time than standard employees. For example, the Bureau of Labor Statistics' contingent work supplement to the Current Population Survey showed that the average wage of contingent employees was 67 percent that of standard employees, and that 30.3 percent of contingent employees worked part time, versus 15.6 percent of standard employees.

At least as troubling as the aforementioned data are the patterns with respect to benefits. One of the standard motivations of firms to employ contingent workers is to save on the costs of employee benefits. Because these workers are on a different payroll than standard employees, the "client" employer is not subject to ERISA (Employee Retirement Income Security Act) and IRS (Internal Revenue Service) non-discrimination requirements to offer benefits more broadly than just to the higher-paid group. The consequences of this are evident in table 2.4: contingent employees are far less likely than regular employees to receive benefits. It is important to note that this is not due to the possibility that they are covered by someone else's (e.g., a spouse's) benefits. For example, only 48 percent of agency "temps" have health insurance from any source.[25]

The main implication we draw from the data is that labor-market policies and institutions ought to assume that employment relationships are and will continue to be more tenuous and less certain in duration than they were in the past. The data do not support, nor do we predict, that all or even most workers in will behave like nomads or "free agents" unattached to stable jobs or employers. Indeed, we are reluctant to make a firm prediction as to whether the trends toward reduced tenure will continue, accelerate, or level off, and we believe it would be prudent for labor-market policy makers and institutions to be equally agnostic about the future. What is clear is that mobility is now,

Table 2.4
Consequences of contingent work (based Susan Houseman's 1999 analysis of the 1997 Current Population Survey contingent worker supplement).

Health insurance

	From any source	Through employer	Eligible from employer
Agency temps	48.1%	7.3%	23.8%
On call	68.5%	20.0%	29.6%
Independent contractors	74.6%	NA[a]	NA
Contract company employees	83.1%	51.3%	68.7%
Regular employees	85.8%	63.9%	75.0%

Pension

	Covered by employer pension plan or has tax-deferred retirement account	Participates in employer plan	Eligible to participate in employer plan
Agency temps	18.3%	4.3%	9.5%
On call	37.0%	22.2%	25.9%
Independent contractors	39.8%	NA	NA
Contract company employees	50.7%	39.2%	46.3%
Regular employees	62.8%	56.1%	60.7%

a. not applicable

and is likely to be in the future, a more important feature of labor markets and career experiences than it has been. Therefore, policies and institutions that support mobility become more central. As we will suggest in the next chapter, this requires a fundamental rethinking of the reliance that the New Deal policy makers placed on the firm as the institution through which a wide variety of labor-market functions and benefits are provided.

The Increasing Importance of Skill and Learning

A fourth major development in the labor market is that the greater competitive pressure on firms leads to new demands by employers for skill and continuous learning. These demands also pose challenges to labor-market institutions as they are currently configured. The demand for skill is increasing for a variety of reasons, but three explanations stand out: globalization and intensified competition from new entrants into deregulated industries, the spread of computer technologies, and the spread of new work systems. In the next chapter we will lay out the facts regarding globalization; here, suffice it to say that globalization is not the only source of new pressures on companies to upgrade the skills of their employees. In industry after industry, deregulation has opened markets for new competition. This is true in such disparate fields as banking, insurance, telecommunications, trucking, and airlines. In most instances, new competitors enter a market with a younger and lower-cost work force and use technology to gain competitive advantage; they also often redefine the boundaries of existing industries, as has clearly has been the case in telecommunications and financial services.

Statistical research and case studies demonstrate that skill requirements rise in industries and firms that are more computer intensive.[26] A second factor is the spread of the new work systems, described above. These factors put a premium on flexibility, problem solving skills, and teamwork. Again, a variety of studies have documented the positive relationship between implementation of these workplace innovations and the skill demands put on the work force.[27]

The heightened demand for skill places a premium on improving the nation's education and job-training system. It is also interacts with the increasing pace of job change, in that strong skills will be more necessary than ever for success in the labor market. It seems clear that people will need education and training throughout their careers.

The importance of knowledge is also underscored by new competitive conditions that put a premium on learning for both individuals and firms. Indeed, analysts now speak of "knowledge workers" and "knowledge management." Knowledge is particularly important in settings where technologies are changing rapidly. Since often the new knowledge required to adapt to technological changes lies outside a firm, a firm must decide whether to retrain its existing work force, to recruit a new work force with the required knowledge, to acquire new organizations that possess the new technologies and the required knowledge, or to form a strategic alliance or enter into a joint venture in order to gain access to the new knowledge base.

The shift in demand for individuals with high levels of skills required to develop and utilize new technologies should give pause to those who believe in the increasing importance of lifelong learning. Although good data are not available, it is clear that many firms have been simultaneously laying off older white-collar and blue-collar workers whose education and training have not equipped them with the skills now in demand and hiring or searching for a new labor force with state-of-the-art technical and behavioral skills. For example, as IBM shifted from its emphasis away from mainframe computers and related hardware in response to increasing demand for software and systems integration, it laid off the equivalent of nearly half of its peak labor force. Perhaps in less dramatic magnitudes, other large companies in the telecommunications sector and in and related technology-intensive sectors exhibited the same pattern. Moreover, "new economy" companies such as Lycos Systems report[28] the average age of their workers to be 28. Is the American economy destined to undergo similar churning in the future, or will we have the wisdom and creativity to develop institutions capable of meeting the demand for lifelong learning and able to keep more workers' skills current as technological changes render present-day skills obsolete?

The Changing Roles of Unions and Government Regulations

Union membership peaked in the United States in the mid 1950s at about 35 percent of the work force. After a period of incremental decline, a sharp decline in membership began in the 1980s. In the private sector, union membership has now returned to about the level it was at just before the New Deal: slightly under 10 percent.

A number of factors account for the decline in union membership. The substantial literature on this subject suggests four interrelated causes: occupational shifts from blue-collar to white-collar or managerial work and shifts from industrial manufacturing to service and knowledge-intensive industries, intensified employer opposition to unions through policies that substitute for union functions and direct suppression of organizing efforts, labor law's inadequacy and its failure to protect workers who try to form unions, and the slowness of unions to adapt to all these challenges and changes.[29]

The decline of unions has had substantial consequences for the operation of the job market. Economists studying why wage inequality has increased attribute a substantial role to it,[30] because unions increase the earnings of those toward the bottom of the wage distribution and also narrow the distribution of earnings within firms that are organized. Another consequence of the weakening of unions is that employees have been frustrated in their efforts to have a more substantial say in how their workplaces are organized.

Furthermore, the loss of union power has led to a compensating increase in government regulations aimed at meeting some of the needs that were traditionally accomplished by unions. We regard the increase in regulations as a second-best solution.

As unions declined, society turned to government regulation as an engine of social regulation of employment standards and outcomes. The New Deal labor and employment system assumed that unions would serve as a strong countervailing force capable of advancing workers' interests and improving on government-established minimum standards for wages and selected working conditions. Indeed, as we will discuss in more detail in later chapters, this was essentially how things worked from the 1930s through the 1950s. Then, as unions gradually declined between 1960 and 1980, government regulation expanded considerably to cover employment outcomes such as safety and health, equal opportunity, pension security, and a host of more specific regulatory requirements. One study found that the number of regulations enforced by the US Department of Labor increased from about 44 to more than 200 during this period.[31]

By most international standards, American employers are still confronted with fewer direct regulations of employment conditions than employers in other countries. However, the shift toward government policy represents a significant departure from the vision of the architects of the New Deal labor policies and the institutional economists who supported and nurtured them through World War II and the postwar years. They envisioned the spread of a system of "industrial jurisprudence" supported by a jointly negotiated and administered grievance procedure as a means of ensuring that the rights and obligations of workers and employer would be enforced flexibly in view of the different circumstances of different workplaces. This would contribute to the goal of industrial democracy, and it would avoid what they feared would be government regulations uninformed by the different norms and operational needs found in different industries and work settings.[32] Two problems arose, however, that limited the realization of this vision. The first was the decline in union membership. The second was that the courts found that, even in unionized settings, arbitrators could not be relied on to protect workers' rights embodied in public laws and (in view of the discriminatory practices that were sometimes embodied in union and non-union practices) could not be relied on to adequately protect the rights of minorities and women to equal employment opportunities or (later) to deal with concerns about sexual harassment. As a result, the courts began to assert more direct jurisdiction over the enforcement of rights embodied in public laws, and they refused to defer to arbitrators chosen by labor and management for their expertise in interpreting the provisions of collective bargaining contracts. In effect, this created a second layer of industrial jurisprudence operating through these administrative agencies and the courts—a jurisprudence aimed not at promoting a general form of industrial democracy or jurisprudence for all workers but at protecting and enforcing specific rights written into laws covering protected categories of workers (e.g., women, older workers, veterans, minorities, the disabled).

The net effect of the shift toward more direct government regulation has been to increase the number of cases referred to government agencies and the courts for resolution.[33] The decline in resources allocated by the Executive Branch and by Congress since 1980 has exacerbated the tensions and delays associated with enforcement. In 1995, for example, the Equal Employment Opportunity Commission reported that more than 100,000 cases were backlogged and awaiting resolution.[34] Moreover, because most lawyers work on contingency fees and settlement levels are normally proportional to one's income, many lower-wage employees have little or no effective access to these services. The courts are also frustrated by the increase in labor and employment cases they are asked to resolve, and they are constantly encouraging government agencies and private parties to develop alternative settlement procedures.

Considerable experimentation with alternative dispute-resolution procedures is underway within private companies and some agencies. Indeed, the Equal Employment Opportunity Commission has cut its backlog in half through use of a voluntary mediation procedure.[35] There is a lively debate underway as to whether these alternative procedures are serving the public interest; we will take this up in chapter 6. The main question to be addressed in regard to updating public policies and institutions is this: How might private institutional arrangements be made to complement public-policy initiatives to achieve the objectives society has set for the workplace while allowing for the flexibility employers are asking for to meet their varied circumstances and while ensuring that all workers have access to enforcement of their rights?

The Persistence of Low-Wage Labor Markets

So far in this chapter we have emphasized changes in labor markets. But there is a persistent and deep problem plaguing the American labor market that also deserves special attention, and we believe it must be given a high priority on any agenda of policy and institutional reform. It is the problem of the persistence of low-wage jobs and labor markets and persistent inequality of income and job opportunities experienced by those left behind by the "new economy."

The labor market has become increasingly divided, and, despite the long boom in employment, poverty rates have been surprisingly stable. In 1989, 13.1 percent of families were below the poverty line; in 1999, the percentage was 11.8. The poverty rate for individuals under 18 was 16.9 percent in 1999. This persistence, which is clearly linked to wage inequality, signals that the low-wage labor market has maintained its significance. How to address the problems of low-wage workers who remain trapped despite economic good times is a major question.

It is convenient but misleading to speak of the low-skill labor market as if it were all of one piece. Consider, for example, the differences between a suburban movie theater with ticket-taker jobs, a garment-industry sweat shop, a hospital hiring orderlies, a downtown department store, and a factory hiring unskilled laborers. Each of these employers may well pay about $8 an hour, yet the working conditions, mobility prospects, skill requirements, and characteristics of the employees will differ substantially.

At one end of the low-wage labor market are the jobs that are below the level of prevailing labor standards. These are often held by undocumented migrants, 6 million of whom are estimated to be living in the United States.[36] In 2000 the *New York Times* reported the following: "The Labor Department estimates that in the San Francisco area more than half the 2000 garment shops violate wage laws. And New York City has more than 3000 apparel sweatshops with more than 50,000 workers, according to a General Accounting Office study. In El Paso, Los Angeles, and Seattle sweatshops are often common."[37] Other classic employers in the low-wage labor market are building cleaning contractors. In 1997, according to Howard Wial, 4.3 percent of wage and salary workers earned less than the minimum wage.[38]

Other employers in the low-wage, low-skill labor market, including fast-food restaurants and movie theaters, operate well within the law and often hire young people for part-time after-school work or for summer jobs. The mobility prospects of these jobs may be limited; however, most of the employees are only passing through, and it is not clear that there are substantial public policy concerns. Intermediate between these extremes are the many low-wage employers in manufacturing, in retail, and in services (e.g., health care) that hire adults, pay at or just above the minimum wage. For their employees, the work may well be a long-term trap.

We can get a rough sense of the magnitude of the low-wage labor market by looking at the earnings of full-time employees. In 1998, of the individuals between ages 25 and 64 who worked full time and year round, 9,772,000 (11.3 percent) earned less than $8.50 an hour.[39] This, of course, is an underestimate of the size of the low-wage, low-skill labor market, since it excludes part-time workers; however, it has the virtue of controlling for age (eliminating young workers) and for individuals' decisions about how many hours to work.

Looked at one way, low-wage jobs, though perhaps not desirable on their own terms, are the first step on a ladder leading to better things. Low-wage employment might provide valuable training, or perhaps the experience of working simply pays off over time. Looked at another way, these are dead-end jobs, and those who enter the low-wage, low-skill labor market as adults are trapped.

The most useful source of data on what happens to adults who work in the low-wage, low-skill sector is the Panel Survey on Income Dynamics. Data from this survey are representative of the entire population, and they allow researchers to compute mobility rates over reasonably long stretches (whereas the Current Population Survey is limited to one-year intervals).

Researchers working with these data come to generally similar conclusions. For example, Osterman found that 49.2 percent of men who were in the bottom earnings quintile in 1979 remained in that quintile in 1995.[40] Although there is clearly mobility, that is a long time for nearly half the group to remain at the bottom. Sawhill and Condon report a 5-year rate of mobility out of the bottom quintile of 47 percent for the period 1979–1986.[41] Gottschalk reports that, between 1968 and 1991, 53.3 percent of those in the bottom quintile moved up.[42] Of those who did move up, nearly half moved only to the second quintile. In short, for a substantial fraction of adults the low-wage, low-skill labor market is not a staging area but a final destination.

The prevailing argument in policy circles today is that low-wage workers' access to and investments in training and education should be increased. This was the dominant theme of the section on low-wage work in the Secretary of Labor's 1999 Labor Day Report (titled Futurework). Clearly, expanding investments, access, and take-up of education and training to low-income workers and families are necessary steps. But we see them as insufficient. A comprehensive and effective strategy for upgrading low-wage jobs and workers should incorporate a mix of policy and institutional changes that address education and training, but it also should incorporate changes in the minimum wage, an earned income tax credit, access to union representation, and initiatives to support the needs of low-wage working parents and their children.

Have Employees Accepted the New Realities?

How have employees reacted to the changes described in this chapter? A few national surveys have asked questions related to this issue, but those questions have not been asked in a systematic way.

The instrument that comes closest to capturing employees' views is the National Survey of the Changing Workforce, conducted by the Families and Work Institute and administered by the polling firm Louis Harris and Associates to a representative national sample in 1997.[43] This survey asked a range of questions about conditions at work and the changing nature of family and work relations. Two questions in particular explored expectations about employment security, an important element of the social contract at work. In the first of these questions, respondents were asked to agree or disagree with the statement "Workers today should not expect a company or organization to provide a lifetime job." Fifty percent of the respondents agreed and 50 percent disagreed with this statement, which concerns what ought to be rather than what actually is employers' commitment to the provision of job security. The second relevant question approached the issue from a slightly different angle, asking about the employee's own expectations for job security in his or her career. The respondents were asked to agree or disagree with the statement "When I first started working, I imagined I would spend my working life mostly with one company or organization." Amazingly, the responses to this question were also evenly split. Even when the sample is distributed in a two-by-two matrix representing the answers to both questions (table 2.5), the

Table 2.5
Combined responses to social-contract questions.

		Workers today should expect a lifetime job.	
		Yes	No
I expected to stay with one employer when I started working.	Yes	26%	25%
	No	23%	26%

response rates are nearly identical. In examining employees'
expectations, it is helpful to focus on the first row of the matrix.
The left cell of the first row (representing affirmative responses to
both questions) in many ways represents those employees who
believe in the "old" social contract—who not only expected to
stay with one employer but also expect that employer to provide
a job that will last a lifetime. Whose responses fall into this cell?
Union members, individuals with a high school education or less,
government employees, parents, blue-collar and technical workers, and long-tenure employees. The right cell of the top row represents the responses of employees who did not agree that
workers should expect a lifetime job but who did expect to stay
with one employer. If there is any evidence that the expectation
of a social contract has been broken from the perspective of the
employee, it should be found in this group. On average, these
workers are more likely to have lost a job as a result of downsizing in the past 5 years, to be older, to have lower income, to be
married, to live in rural areas, and to work in older industries
(e.g., communications, transportation, utilities). Although these
two questions pertain to only one dimension of the social contract, and although they do so in a superficial way, they provide
another indication that efforts to update labor-market policies
and institutions ought to cope with these variations in employee
expectations.

The data suggest that employees' expectations are more
resilient than the popular rhetoric would have us believe. Despite
downsizing and the rhetoric about the need for employees to
take responsibility for their own career security, about half the
labor force continues to expect employers to provide long-term
career-oriented jobs.[44]

Data collected by David Levine and colleagues[45] are consistent
with the stability in expectations suggested here. Using data from
1984–85 and 1995, Levine et al. compared employees' judg-

ments of fairness with respect to layoffs. Levine et al. found no significant shift in views across this time period as to when a layoff or a pay cut would be perceived as fair. Layoffs that occur in profitable firms and pay cuts that take advantage of the existence of a supply of workers who would accept a lower wage continue to be viewed as unfair by a majority of workers, even in the heart of Silicon Valley. We should keep these employees' views in mind as we consider strategies for rebuilding labor-market institutions that can meet these expectations of employees.

Summary and Conclusions

When thoughtful people consider the record of the 1990s, they notice the juxtaposition of increasing employment and declining unemployment with stagnant wages and worsening inequality. They are right to notice this, and we share their concern with the darker side of the labor market. The labor market has become increasingly bifurcated. Worsening inequality in wages is a reflection of this underlying characteristic of the job market. Despite the prosperity of recent years, the low-wage labor market not only has persisted but shows signs of growth. A substantial portion of the work force seems trapped in bad jobs and able to experience the "new economy" only through media reports.

Other developments occurring in the job market are more positive. We have highlighted how the traditional boundaries between occupations, particularly those between what blue-collar workers do and what managers do, have dissolved. There is now much more overlap and ambiguity in occupational roles, and this creates new challenges for management, for the legal framework of governing the labor market, and for the skill-acquisition system. And the nature of careers have changed. There is now much more mobility, both voluntary and involuntary, than there once was. In addition, the nature of the attachment between employers and employees has changed, and the emergence of contingent jobs has challenged traditional notions of employment.

The increased complexity and diversity of the labor market poses a particularly difficult challenge. Changes in who is working have put more pressure on families, and any effort to reconstruct labor-market institutions must take this into account. Firms are also experiencing new pressures that put a premium on their ability to operate flexibly in the face of changing technologies, globalization, and newly competitive product markets. Finally, unions—a key mediating institution—have experienced a long-term decline, among the consequences of which have been declining earnings, increased government regulation of the workplace, and the inability of employees to have as much of a voice in the workplace as they desire.

An increasingly varied and diverse labor market requires institutions that are flexible and responsive to different circumstances, yet today's labor-market institutions were created in an era of much more uniformity and stability. Behind some of these changes is the growing premium that both employers and employees place on obtaining more flexibility in a rapidly changing competitive environment and a fluid labor market. Yet our labor-market institutions have only partially adapted to the need for greater flexibility and to the shifts in the labor market. Stagnating earnings, work-family conflicts, increasing litigation, and inequality are consequences of the failure to change. We cannot rely entirely on strong macroeconomic performance to solve these problems.

3

The Corporation in the Labor Market

In this chapter we will examine changes in the structure and in the role of the American corporation and how these changes affect employment relations. As we stated in chapter 1, many of the policies and the institutions of the American labor market were designed around a view of the corporation as it existed during and immediately after the New Deal era. On this view, corporations were highly integrated, performing a wide range of functions within clear boundaries, and they offered stable, long-term employment at predictable wages and with basic benefits. Thus, a variety of labor-market institutions and practices were built around the corporation.

Changes in the competitive environment since the New Deal era have undermined the corporation as it was seen in the past. The new business model is distinguished from the New Deal version by the following:

• a significant reduction in the functional focus of the firm—firms are now more focused on their "core competencies," and hence they are "outsourcing" many services and functions that they once performed internally

• a focus on flexibility, speed, and innovation, including the rapid shifting of the corporation's business scope from one product area or market to another

• the deployment of assets and operations around the globe

• fierce competition for scarce "knowledge workers," often entailing incentive-based wages and various stock options, at the expense of more traditional semi-skilled manufacturing and clerical employees.

Owing to these changes, the American corporation, around which many of the current labor-market institutions and policies were designed, is constantly restructuring its activities and revisiting its decisions regarding what to "buy" rather than "make" and how to maintain its viability in a highly competitive and turbulent market. Even more notable is the increasing variation in the organizational design of American firms. No longer can public policy assume, as it did in the New Deal era, that a single model is dominant or will become dominant. In view of the increased variety of organizational forms, policies based on a unitary conception of the corporation cannot be effective in today's economy. In this chapter we discuss these changes and their implications for the world of work.

From the New Deal to the New Economy

In the eyes of policy makers of the New Deal era, the prototypical employer was a large, integrated industrial corporation seeking to grow to a size suitable to the expanding domestic market. Capital was the most critical resource for the corporation. Indeed, the ability to pool large amounts of capital gave rise to the emergence of the corporation in the late nineteenth century and the early twentieth century. According to the business model of the New Deal era, competitive advantage was achieved through gains in productivity, which were often due to advances in technology and increases in economy of scale as well as to superior marketing and distribution. Firms with lower unit costs and stronger brand recognition would capture the imaginations and the dollars of American consumers. Competition was among a limited number of large, primarily domestic corporations. Through the widespread use of industry and community wage surveys (and, in some industries, pattern bargaining—that is, a stable wage relationship across firms and industries), wages were "taken out of competition." Instead, American corporations sought to capture greater shares of the market through incremental product innovation, price leadership, and extensive advertising.

The architects of the New Deal accepted the view that the corporation and its management should be accountable to shareholder interests.[1] But while maximizing shareholder wealth gradually came to be seen as the primary objective of the American firm, neither the American public nor those who made public policy ever viewed it as the sole responsibility of the corporation. As New Deal policy makers considered the labor market, they gave firms additional responsibilities. Firms were to fulfill these responsibilities either by complying with minimum standards specified by law or by negotiating with countervailing institutions (such as unions) that were encouraged and protected by law. Specifically, two important bodies of social-welfare policy and employment policy were enacted that made individual firms the central institution through which employees' needs for long-term income security would be met and the forum in which employees would negotiate improvements in their wages, hours, and working conditions. The Social Security Act and the Fair Labor Standards Act set minimum labor standards and created social-welfare programs that were inteded to protect all workers and to provide for them upon retirement or if they lost their jobs temporarily (owing to layoff) or permanently (owing to disability). The National Labor Relations Act (better known as the Wagner Act, after Senator Robert Wagner of New York) established collective bargaining as a means for helping employees to amass enough countervailing power to improve on the minimum conditions set by the other acts and to tailor collective bargaining to the needs of specific workplaces.

As unions grew in size and in bargaining power, they began to include health insurance and other benefits in their bargaining agendas. In 1949 the Supreme Court ruled that pensions were a "mandatory" subject of bargaining and thus encouraged negotiators to expand the array of benefits (health insurance, pensions, disability protections, sick leave, etc.) covered in collective bargaining.

These policies and bargaining strategies carried over from the earlier period of welfare capitalism the idea that the individual firm should be both the central unit around which employment relations should be built and governed and the conduit for delivering a variety of social-welfare and labor-market sources.[2] Large firms could efficiently purchase health insurance and build pension reserves for their employees that would supplement Social Security. Because firms were assumed to be stable and employment relationships were presumed to be of long duration, the funding of social security, unemployment insurance, and other benefits could be tied to the firm and financed through payroll taxes.[3] This combination of policies and institutional arrangements would allow firms to exploit their expanding markets, would ensure labor and social stability, and would keep the economy on the road to a more equitably shared prosperity. It also laid the groundwork for the gradual emergence of an implicit social contract between American workers and employers. Marina Whitman, formerly chief economist at General Motors, summarized this old social contract succinctly:

Four words sum up the old social contract, as most American understood it: *permanence* in the employer-employee relationship, producing long-term job security and mutual commitment; *entitlement* not only to a job but also to a steady pay advancement and generous benefits, for all employees who performed adequately and didn't violate company policies; *paternalism,* in the form of a shared view of employees as part of a company 'family'; and *hierarchy,* such that lines of authority and levels of status were clearly defined within the firm and carried over to the outside world.[4]

Thus, gradually over the 40 years that followed the passage of the New Deal legislation, firms came to be relied on as the institution that would provide, either on their own or through collective bargaining, secure long-term jobs and careers, private reserves for retirement, health insurance for workers and their families, and training and education to build human capital.

Although this image of the New Deal corporation may have been a reasonably accurate caricature of large firms, it never captured the reality of employment relations in many of the smaller enterprises. Indeed, during the New Deal period, as today, about 55 percent of the work force was employed in establishments (i.e., work sites) with fewer than 50 employees. Then, as now, about one-third of the labor force worked in firms with fewer than 50 employees. Employment practices and outcomes varied widely among small firms and establishments. Those that were unionized and engaged in multi-employer bargaining could likewise "take wages of out competition" and pool resources to pay high wages and fund benefits at levels comparable to those of larger employers. Some small firms that remained privately owned were led and managed in a paternalistic fashion, with employees treated as family members and with many welfare benefits and labor-market functions provided informally. Many, however, paid lower wages and provided fewer benefits and thus experienced higher turnover and were less able to attract and retain the most talented workers. As a result, size of firm and unionization are the two best predictors of the quality of employment outcomes provided by employers in the post-New Deal years.[5]

Pressures for a New Business Model

Increased globalization and technological innovation have radically changed the competitive environment for American firms large and small. Markets have become simultaneously globalized and segmented, while a combination of new technologies and deregulation have provided opportunities for individual firms, sometimes entire industries, to experiment with alternative business strategies and structures. Together, these developments have undermined the business model of the New Deal era.

Globalization

Global trade and global capital mobility increased dramatically in the last two decades of the twentieth century. For example, trade among the industrial democracies grew at almost twice the rate of total economic output during the 1970s and the 1980s.[6] Whereas global trade amounted to about one-third of total world output in the early 1970s, it approached 45 percent in 1995. Intra-industry trade, an indication of competition within similar product markets, far outstripped inter-industry trade, thus heightening competition among producers for similar markets. At the same time, world trade has become progressively less dominated by exchanges within the OECD nations since various newly industrialized countries and OPEC countries increased their exports after the oil crisis of the late 1970s. In 1990, imports from Brazil, Hong Kong, Mexico, Singapore, South Korea, and Taiwan constituted almost 10 percent of total OECD imports by the United States.[7] If exports from the OPEC countries were to be added, this share would grow even more.

These trends increased in the 1990s, and they had dramatic consequences for the American economy. Whereas exports plus imports constituted only 11 percent of GDP in 1970, this percentage rose to 26 in 1997.[8] This 150 percent growth in trade, a strong indicator of the international integration of national economies, completely changed the competitive climate of American companies. Whereas before American companies saw their competition as primarily domestic, in the 1980s and the 1990s they came to understand that some of their most aggressive challengers were international companies. Even if, as Paul Krugman argues, American companies continue to produce primarily for the domestic market, that market has become increasingly targeted and fought over by non-American companies. Either through exports from home-base operations or through foreign direct investment in the United States, these international firms have sought, often successfully, to capture ever-greater shares of the enormous consumer market of the United States.

Financial integration and movement of capital across borders also increased dramatically in these years. For example, international bank lending grew from around $200 billion in 1973 to almost $4 trillion in 1992.[9] Between 1979 and 1990, cross-border equity flows also increased rapidly, exceeding $1600 billion in 1990.[10] And annual inflows of foreign direct investment increased almost tenfold since the late 1970s, climbing to $185 billion in 1989.[11] Although the raw numbers on international capital flow are staggering, some economists, including those working at the International Monetary Fund, believe that the best indicator of capital mobility is the existence of government restrictions on international capital movements. But even if this more restrictive measure is used, the changes are still impressive. In the early 1970s, less than 15 percent of countries had no capital controls. By the mid 1990s, about 30 percent of countries had removed controls on capital mobility. This trend continued into the 1990s, especially in Europe after the enactment of the Single European Act in the 1990s.

In short, although there is significant debate on the origins and the consequences of globalization, there can be no doubt that consequent changes in capital and product markets have fundamentally changed the competitive environment for American corporations and thus had profound consequences for various categories of American workers.

Technological Innovation

Technological innovation, especially in information and communication technologies, has also dramatically affected the competitive environment of American firms. By reducing communication costs, information technology (IT) has had the dual consequence of enhancing the specialization of individual firms while leading to their disaggregation. For example, access to a global customer base through the Internet makes it worthwhile for individual firms to specialize in a narrow product line or service (à la Adam Smith's pin factory). As firms specialize, inter-firm relationships begin to substitute for intra-firm relations along a chain of production. This, in turn, leads to the disaggregation of previously integrated firms and to the emergence of highly competitive specialized firms. As specialization becomes increasingly competitive, firms do less "in house" and instead do more outsourcing or partnering with other firms.

Besides affecting intra-firm relations and the boundaries of individual firms, innovations in IT have supported the reorganization of work within the firm. Layers of middle managers who previously performed various communication and coordination roles (among other things) have been eliminated as new information systems have been introduced within American firms. The increased importance of IT systems to company competitiveness has also raised the premium for skilled knowledge workers.

Although we consider technology an important driver of change, it is important to recognize that firms continue to have choices as to whether they use technology to upgrade workers' skills and enhance customer service or to segment the labor force and their customer base. Studies of the telecommunications industry[12] and of the banking industry[13] have shown that both strategies are being followed. The "high-road" (i.e., high-skills, high-technology) option clearly achieves more joint gains for shareholders, customers, and employees than the more segmented strategy. Which will dominate is a critical question for decision makers inside firms and those in the investor and labor-market policy communities who seek to monitor and/or influence the behavior of firms.

More recently, innovations in IT have helped to create industries that deliver traditional services in new ways. "E-commerce"—the use of various Internet-based means of marketing, ordering, and purchasing items as diverse as software, groceries, books, lectures, and automobiles—is having a profound effect on the competitive dynamics of many industries and on the nature of the employment relationships governing the firms and workers involved. While posing competitive threats to many existing firms, these new ways of competing and the new firms they are spawning are creating exciting and challenging opportunities for workers with the skills, the ability, and the willingness to take the risks associated with working in a startup organization.

Deregulation

Since the late 1970s, deregulation of various industries has also led to an increased rate of entry of new firms with lower costs than existing competitors that carry costs associated with older work forces and comprehensive benefit structures associated with the New Deal and postwar social contract. The effects of deregulation are particularly profound in industries where there are low barriers to entry, such as in trucking. Since 1978, when the trucking industry was deregulated, large numbers of new firms and owner-operated truckers have entered the industry and have introduced a new wave of price and service competition.

The results have been a decline in unionization from 60 percent in 1977 to 20 percent in 1995 and a decline in real wages of about 30 percent over this time period (nearly 4 times as large a decline as for the average hourly worker across all industries).[14] Similar declines in unionization and in wages were experienced in the segments of the telecommunications industry that experienced the most new entrants. Union membership in telecommunications declined from 55 percent in 1983 to 29 percent in 1996. The biggest effect of deregulation on wages in this industry was to increase wage inequality, particularly among clerical and sales workers; new non-union entrants set wages for these workers as much as 25 percent below the rates provided in union contracts. Overall, real wages declined 20 percent for non-union clerical and sales workers and 12 percent for non-union technical workers between 1983 and 1996.[15] The exceptions to this deregulation effect appear to be the airline and railroad industries, in which few new entrants have survived and unionization remains at about the same high levels it was at before deregulation. Relative wages have declined somewhat in these industries, but not as dramatically as in industries in which deregulation also produced big declines in union coverage.

Power Shifts: Investor Capitalism on the Rise
In addition to these changes in markets and technologies, a profound shift in corporate governance has reshaped the strategies and the structures of many American companies, especially companies that are publicly traded. Michael Useem describes the 1980s and the 1990s as the era of "investor capitalism."[16] The risk of hostile takeovers, made possible by a willingness to use highly leveraged capital instruments, opened an era in which institutional investors became more powerful in pressuring and controlling management and demanding larger and quicker returns. This has created a set of incentives for companies that

undermine the countervailing power of employees. At one time, American corporations would lay off employees only during downturns in the business cycle; today, many firms with strong performance will nonetheless lay off employees to send signals to the capital markets and to improve their stocks' trading prices.

In summary, changes in the external environment and new opportunities offered by technology have radically altered the business model upon which most traditional American firms were organized. In contrast with the large, vertically integrated structures of the past, firms today are advised to focus their energies and resources on their "core competencies" and to look for opportunities to outsource all other services or functions to specialized companies or contractors. Speed, flexibility, and development of new products and services have become the critical competitive strategies. As a result, concerns for workforce stability and labor peace have been supplanted with concerns for attracting and retaining employees who have the knowledge and skills to use emerging technologies to create and deliver new products and services. Compensation principles emphasize pay-for-performance arrangements for core employees in an effort to better align employees' and owners' interests and to create incentives for these employees to stay with the firm. Finally, in view of the global nature of today's markets, flexibility to deploy assets and locate operations wherever necessary takes on greater importance. Variations in labor cost and the need to be close to markets are leading to global dispersion of production and service operations and to more cross-border alliances, mergers, and acquisitions. The one thing that may not have changed is the presumed advantage of size. The consolidation of firms within industries (or across industry lines that share complementary technologies, such as telecommunications and cable TV) appears to continue apace today—much as in the early years of the twentieth century, when many large manufacturing and transportation firms consolidated.

Between Old and New: American Corporations Struggle to Adapt

The preceding brief overview provides a backdrop to the challenges that face managers, employees, and their representatives as they seek to adapt their structures, strategies, and employment relations to the current environment. In this subsection we will explore the various ways firms have attempted to adapt to these changes, using the experiences of a number of well-known firms to illustrate how both firms that evolved out of the New Deal era and emerging firms are attempting to address these challenges. Wherever possible (although the research evidence is still in a nascent stage), we will juxtapose older firms with firms of more recent vintage. The examples will illustrate the tremendous variation in organizational forms and settings that now characterizes the labor market—a variation that our institutions will have to accommodate. We will begin by comparing the human-resources strategies of two prototypical firms operating in the same industry: Lucent Technologies and Cisco Systems.

Cisco Systems

Perhaps no company better illustrates the new business model and organizational form and its implications for employment relations than Cisco Systems, a rapidly growing high-technology firm that specializes in designing networking systems that link computers and provide Internet communications. Cisco is a leader in the development of data communications switching technologies and a major competitor of Lucent Technologies, a firm that retains many features of its New Deal heritage. Cisco, founded in 1990, has grown rapidly in size, profits, and stock value. It contracts (or "partners") with outside firms for most of its manufacturing. It has grown mostly through acquisition, purchasing more than 40 companies during the first 9 years of its life.

From its inception, Cisco focused on finding and bringing in the intellectual capital it needed to build its core business; it had support functions that it deemed to be outside its core competencies performed by partner firms. Vice President of Human Resources Barbara Beck described this strategy in an interview in early 1999:

Technology is changing so fast we can't develop it all. So we fill out our development with acquisitions, especially when a new technology is emerging that might now or in the future fit in with or enhance our products. . . .

Along with this strategy of growth through acquisition and this focus on state-of-the-art technology, Cisco aggressively recruits and tries to retain valued knowledge workers. Says Barbara Beck:

. . . We also hire knowledge workers to transform industries. Our company philosophy is to share rewards and risks. We pay low base salaries—about 65 percent of the industry average. Bonuses are paid on the basis of firm performance relative to the industry and on customer satisfaction. All employees receive stock options when they are hired and receive additional options based on their performance. Forty percent of the outstanding stock options are held by non-managerial employees. The options represent a substantial amount of money, since Cisco's stock has increased over 500 percent and has split at least once in its history.

According to Beck, Cisco does not want to be a "model employer" for every type of worker; rather, it wants to be a model employer for those who match its organizational culture:

I don't believe you can generalize our relationship to all companies because we are so selective in hiring people who can make a difference here. We want to make Cisco a great place to work for people who want to work here—those who fit into Cisco's culture.

Currently, Cisco utilizes about 2300 agency temporary employees and 800 contractors. In view of the laws governing these contingent relationships, the management of these relationships poses difficult problems. Again, Barbara Beck:

The laws on this were designed for an industrial age. Now companies like ours manage differently. We have a high level of uncertainty in the number of new hires we need to make in any period and we only want to hire people we know we will not have to lay off. So we use contingents to buffer the uncertainty and variability in demand. Moreover, lots of people want to work for multiple companies. For example, we use independent contractors as recruiters. These people are great—they are effective in finding the right people for us and they don't want to become regular employees. We also bring in people to do specific project work— peak jobs that we are not sure will last beyond the project. But the tax law, and the recent Microsoft case are forcing us to redefine some of these people either as temporary employees (they have to now go through an agency) or as regular employees. So we put in 'gates' to decide who belongs in which category, and many of these people are very unhappy about losing their contractor status. This is a major source of frustration for us and for these people. Many want the flexibility.

Thus, Cisco is an example of a recently emerged high-technology Silicon Valley firm that is benefiting from rapid growth and from human-resources policies of the sort that rapid growth and rapidly increasing profits can support. It has developed a niche, in which it promotes innovation by providing an environment conducive to attracting and retaining knowledge workers. In fact, Cisco's core competency is the technology and the people it develops and acquires. Its compensation system is designed to align the incentives of its workers with those of its shareholders and its customers. Cisco recruits and selects individuals who are attracted and can contribute to this culture and to the shared vision of "transforming" an industry through their products and technologies. The company's fantastic growth and profitability reinforce its culture, keep turnover low by industry standards, and have made a large number of its employees very wealthy.

Cisco's success depends on its ability to keep its technologies—which define its markets—at the edge of innovation. It constantly looks for growth opportunities, and it hedges against missing technical developments by using its resources to purchase firms for their technical and human assets. It provides its employees with a challenging environment in which there are opportunities for continuous learning for those individuals willing to commit to the corporate culture of entrepreneurialism, long hours of work, and risk taking. It provides a host of services, including auto repair and pickup and delivery of dry cleaning, to support its employees' commitment to working the long hours they often must put in to meet deadlines.

Lucent Technologies

Lucent Technologies, Inc., created in 1994 by the breakup of AT&T, consists of Bell Labs' and AT&T's former network systems development and manufacturing businesses. Lucent designs, manufactures, and services public and private networks, systems, and software, data networking systems, business telephone systems, and microelectronic equipment. Lucent's research and development function is performed by Bell Labs.

Lucent is in direct competition with Cisco Systems and is engaged in a similar effort to develop and/or purchase the technologies that will dominate the next generation of data transfer and networking. Unlike Cisco, however, Lucent has an installed base of approximately 49,000 employees who manufacture, install, and service its products, and these employees are represented by two important and powerful unions: the Communications Workers of America and the International Brotherhood of Electrical Workers. The generally good relationship between the company and its unions goes back to the AT&T years. Like Cisco, Lucent is under strong pressure to allocate capital resources to R&D and/or to purchase companies with promising technologies, and the executives of its various business units are likewise under pressure to develop and deliver new products to various markets quickly and at low cost. In addition, Lucent must compete with Cisco and other firms that contract out most of their manufacturing and installation work. This creates considerable uncertainty and considerable conflict between the company's overall desire for good labor-management relations and the individual executives' incentives to outsource some if not all of this work

Lucent's strategy for catching up to competitors such as Cisco has been to acquire companies that have strengths in certain areas of emerging technology and to sell other units that are not essential to its core business. "When we buy these firms," a Lucent human-resources executive said, "we are buying the technology and the people, and we have to make sure we don't lose the key people. How to do it? They don't want to work for a big bureaucratic company. They don't expect to stay with one company for 30 years so a pension is meaningless. They want a 401(k) and equity-stock options."[17]

However, for Lucent's hourly employees the future is full of challenges and uncertainty. The primary threat lies in the fact that most of Lucent's competitors, and Cisco Systems in particular, outsource their manufacturing operations to smaller firms with significantly lower costs. This puts pressure on the leaders of Lucent's business units to do the same. As a result, debates about outsourcing have become the central labor-relations issue for the company and its union leaders. Built into their labor agreements, Lucent and its unions have a procedure for labor-management consultation called "The Workplace of the Future." Carried over from the old AT&T contract, this mechanism is supposed to serve as a means of sharing information on labor-management issues; however, as both company and union leaders acknowledge, it has not worked well, because the executives in charge of the business units are not committed to working with the union leaders and are under strong pressure to emphasize R&D and new-product development. As a result, often they make decisions quickly without consulting national union leaders.

In an interview in early 1999, James Irvine, the top Communications Workers of America leader responsible for relations with Lucent, described the situation as follows:

> The participatory effort is just about to snap apart. Within the past three months, the company did three things without prior consultation with us that indicates they are not serious about a partnership. In September they subcontracted work done by our installations technicians—high-tech work involving the 5E switching machinery—done for Bell System companies. In October they informed us of their intent to franchise out more work done for Bell companies. In November, they informed us they intend to outsource a lot of manufacturing work—there will be no layoffs because there is 17 percent attrition per year, but this will mean a reduction of this many CWA jobs. Again, no discussion—just notification.
>
>   Our members are really angry. . . . They feel there is no loyalty left with Lucent. They have no loyalty to us so we shouldn't give any to them. Workers feel betrayed, especially because the company is doing well and they see the top people at Lucent doing very well. The inequity really gets to them.

Indeed, events since 1999 have not been kind to Lucent's shareholders or its employees. In the wake of a precipitous decline in its stock price, the company replaced its CEO and announced its intent to split into several separate entities. The long-term effects of these actions remain to be seen, but their short-term effects on employee relations are clear: They divide employees by severing the business units with the best growth prospects from those whose employees have good reason to feel insecure and uncertain about their futures. Uncertainty as to what work will be done in house and what work will be done by outside contractors, as to what will happen in the separate entities created by the recent restructuring, and as to Lucent's prospects in the technological race and in the marketplace of the future makes it difficult for management and union leaders to sustain a good labor-management relationship.

In some ways the contrasts between Cisco and Lucent are unique to those firms, but in other ways they are typical of a more general divide between "new economy" firms and "old economy" firms. For example, recent research on "new economy" firms illustrates the centrality of human resources—intellectual capital and the organizational practices needed to mobilize and retain skilled workers—to their success. According to one study, startup firms that assign responsibility for human resources to a human-resources executive are more likely to survive and grow than those that do not.[18] Another study, based on a sample of Silicon Valley startups, shows that firms with human-resources policies that stress employee commitment and employee retention are more likely to be able to go public.[19] Yet many of these new firms are non-union, and almost all of them outsource their manufacturing to subcontractors. As a result, their costs are much lower than those of more traditional American firms, which bear the financial burdens and the social obligations of older and often unionized work forces. This difference makes it extremely difficult for the more established firms to compete with the startups in the same market segments. It also creates incentives for the older firms to renegotiate, or even renege on, their social contract with their employees.

In short, the tension between maintaining a commitment to positive labor-management relations and outsourcing work to the lowest bidder is a constant challenge facing larger, older companies today.

Kodak

The tensions within more traditional corporations and between them and their newer competitors are sometimes exacerbated by the presence or absence or unions. Often, however, the difficulties faced by existing companies have little to do with whether or not their employees are unionized. A good example is the Eastman Kodak Company.

Since the turn of the twentieth century, Eastman Kodak has been one of the most important corporate citizens of Rochester, New York. A leading proponents of welfare capitalism, it paid high wages and provide lifetime job security to its employees well into the 1980s.[20] However, during the 1980s the company embarked on a strategy of diversification and acquisition by purchasing Sterling Drug Company and expanding into a wider range of products, including office copying machines.

As a prototypical, highly integrated firm, Kodak performed all of its own R&D, manufacturing, and sales functions. A 1998 article in the business newspaper *Barrons* echoed the investment community's criticism of the company for maintaining this integration too long:

Many of Kodak's problems stem from the company's remarkable success in the century following its founding in 1892. Unfortunately, as the world changed rapidly over the past 20 years, Kodak remained stuck in its illustrious past. Other world-class companies were adapting to the new realities of business by forming corporate partnerships, joint ventures and close relationships with suppliers. Yet Kodak always took its founder's slogan, 'You press the button and we do the rest' much too far. The company insisted on preserving its self-reliance to the point of making its own screws and springs and sheet metal. Millions of dollars were frittered away on research with no practical application. Damn the costs, Kodak was determined to be an industrial fiefdom in the 19th-century mold.[21]

As Kodak's market position deteriorated in the late 1980s and through the 1990s, lifetime employment and an integrated structure and strategy gave way to periodic downsizing: 3100 workers in 1983, 12,000 in 1986, 6000 in 1989, 3000 in 1991, 19,000 in 1997.[22] When George Fisher was brought in as CEO in 1993, he refocused the company on its core businesses (film and imaging), sold most of its non-core businesses, and entered into a number of a number of joint ventures and partnerships with firms in the imaging and information-services businesses. At the same time, Fisher reaffirmed Kodak's commitment to a new social contract with its employees—one that, though no longer promising lifetime employment, nonetheless involved a high level of mutual commitment on both sides. Unfortunately, events in the marketplace prevented Fisher from achieving these goals. He left Kodak, and the company has continued to reduce its employment level and its commitment to its work force. Hence, the chain of events that this resolutely non-union firm experienced was very similar to what Lucent went through.

It would be easy but wrong to assume that the lessons offered by these examples apply only to manufacturing. There are comparable cases outside the manufacturing sector.

Southwest Airlines

Southwest Airlines may be the prototypical example of a service-sector firm has been phenomenally successful in part because it has organized itself along entirely new lines. Its employees do a wide variety of jobs (pilots sometimes help load baggage), are involved in hiring, and are compensated with various gains-sharing programs. It is also far more successful than most airlines at coordinating relations among different occupational and professional groups—a problem that has long plagued the airline industry.[23]

Southwest Airlines, formed in 1971 to serve three Texas cities, now has about 24,000 employees, serves 25 states, and offers approximately 2500 flights per day. It operates as a low-cost, no-frills, high-customer-service, point-to-point airline, whereas its larger competitors use a hub-and-spoke system. One key to Southwest's success is its low turnaround time (the time required for a plane to land and take off again), which requires a great deal of teamwork and coordination among employees and occupational groups.[24] The company works hard at maintaining a culture that emphasizes flexibility, family orientation, and fun. Its human-resources practices focus on careful recruitment and selection, flexibility, cross-functional and cross-occupational coordination, and good labor-management relations.

Nearly 90 percent of Southwest's workers belong to one of nine unions. The pilots, three small technician unions, the flight attendants, and the ramp workers are represented by the Transportation Workers Unions, the customer-service representatives and the reservation agents by the International Association of Machinists, and the mechanics and the cleaners by the International Brotherhood of Teamsters. Southwest has enjoyed highly cooperative and peaceful labor relations since its founding. Its founders were not opposed to unions and essentially invited them in. But the company has also worked hard to ensure that the unions have the same objectives as the company and thereby to avoid adversarial relations.

Southwest has been highly successful, generating profits each year since it was founded and realizing significant appreciation in the value of its stock. Its quality and its productivity are benchmarks for the industry. It consistently ranks at the top in on-time performance, baggage handling, and customer satisfaction. Although there is no guarantee that this success will go on forever, it does suggest that attention to human-resources practices in service industries can support a virtuous cycle of positive employee relations and outcomes, high customer satisfaction and quality of service, and high returns to shareholders. External investors appear to recognize value in this strategy. Southwest continues to enjoy price/earnings ratios considerably higher than those of its competitors.

The contrast between new players like Southwest Airlines and older, more established players is perhaps best illustrated by a comparison with United Airlines.

United Airlines

In July of 1994, after years of eroding profitability and increasingly difficult labor relations, United Airlines employees represented by the Air Line Pilots Association and by the International Association of Machinists joined with non-union employees to purchase 55 percent of the company. United's flight attendants decided not to participate.

In the first 6 years of the Employee Stock Ownership Plan (ESOP), employee representatives on the board have exerted significant influence on the decision whether to form an alliance with another airline company, on the choice of a CEO and later the choice of his successor, and on the criteria to be used in evaluating and rewarding managers and executives. (United now includes customer satisfaction and employee satisfaction as significant criteria in managerial and executive evaluations.) However, it is not at all clear whether these changes will suffice to maintain the company's competitiveness.

Although United's profits and the value of its stock have both increased since the ESOP was instituted, other airlines have had similar success.[25] Likewise, labor relations are improving as new, interest-based approaches to negotiation are introduced, but there is little evidence that employees enjoy greater involvement and more of a voice in the day-to-day issues that affect them or in issues that influence on-time performance, customer satisfaction, and productivity. The efforts at cultural change have been largely symbolic and incremental rather than systemic. In the case of supervisors, their reductions in number and their changed role may have had negative results. Thus, United has not succeeded in gaining significant value or competitive advantage from its work force, despite its new ownership and governance arrangements.

At the same time, employment security has been maintained, and union representatives have influenced a number of strategic decisions that are of major concern to employees and share-holders. The long-term future of the ESOP depends on how the parties address several critical challenges, including renegotiating their collective bargaining agreements and deciding whether to extend the ESOP's provisions beyond their expiration date. The real issue for United Airlines is not the mechanisms of governance but whether the cost savings and the flexibility gained through the ESOP are enough to offset the financial burdens associated with the company's extensive infrastructure and its commitment to its work force. With high-quality, lower-cost competitors such as Southwest eating away at its market share, it is not at all clear that United and the other more established airlines can continue to compete and maintain social obligations to their work forces.

Common Responses to Common Challenges

In important ways, the case of Lucent vs. Cisco and the case of United vs. Southwest exemplify what happens when "old economy" firms and "new economy" operate in the same industry. There exist many other examples in an array of different industries. The point of our comparisons was not to illustrate the differences between established and newer firms but rather to illustrate the challenges that many established American companies are facing as they seek to balance the competing claims of adapting to a new market environment and maintaining their commitments to their existing work forces. In other words, we chose these cases because we wanted to illustrate that the major divide in the present-day American economy is not between "bad," "lean and mean," "low-road," anti-union companies and "enlightened," "high-road," socially responsible enterprises but between companies with very different business models and cost structures, all in an intensely competitive and unpredictable environment.

In the course of our research we certainly encountered individual firms that appeared to pursue profits at any cost and to show little concern for their employees. But most of the firms we studied—both "old-economy" and "new-economy" firms—wanted to do right by their employees but were genuinely struggling with how to do right while maintaining the levels of economic performance expected of them by their shareholders and by outside investors. In this section we will highlight and illustrate two of the most common responses to these challenges.

Adoption of Knowledge-Based Work Systems

In chapter 2 we noted that major changes in the organization of work have been underway in American industry for several decades. One way to interpret these changes is to see them as efforts to draw more fully on the collective knowledge and skills of the hourly or production-level work force. If knowledge is a critical asset in organizations today, one way to increase the value of employees is to ensure that the knowledge of all employees is being put to work.

At the core of the new systems are changes that give employees more say in how to do their jobs and changes aimed at encouraging greater teamwork, flexibility, and problem solving. Sometimes the new systems involve reorganization of individual jobs into work teams. In many instances these teams are led by management employees, but the role of a management employee in such a position has changed from that of a manager to that of a "coach" or "facilitator." In other instances, teams are self-directed. In many "transformed" firms, employees are involved in things other than direct work activities. In the most common example of this, employees work in groups that include both managerial and non-managerial personnel; the idea here is to mitigate the traditional distinctions. These groups typically address production techniques, quality issues, and matters of health and safety. At the extreme, these groups may take up topics that in the past were considered clearly "managerial," such as outsourcing and supplier policy.

In the early 1990s, although the impression seemed to be that American firms were slow to adopt high-performance work systems, research on the rate of adoption found that about one-fifth and perhaps as many as one-third had adopted substantial elements of those systems.[26] Most likely to adopt these systems were firms with relatively high-skill technologies, firms that competed in international markets, firms that placed a high value on product quality, and large firms with multiple locations.[27] More recent evidence, from a 1997 survey,[28] shows that the diffusion of high-performance work systems continued at a rapid pace and became equally common in union and non-union workplaces.

For the percentage of establishments with each of four practices commonly part of new work systems covering at least 50 percent level of its "core" employees (i.e, employees involved in its central business activities) in 1992 and in 1997, see table 3.1. The data presented in that table point to the power of these ideas and to their surprising ability to flourish even in an era of downsizing and employment insecurity. Only the diffusion of self-managed work teams was restrained. Self-managed work teams are probably the category most affected by layoffs and other radical organizational changes, since they are hard to manage successfully if the personnel keep shifting. In addition, in some respects self-managed work teams represent the biggest threat to established power relationships in the organization. For these reasons, the slower adoption of that practice should not be surprising.

Table 3.1
Percentages of establishments with various high-performance work practices involving at least half of "core" employees (employees involved in the establishment's central business activities). Source: P. Osterman, "Work Organization in an Era of Restructuring: Trends in Diffusion and Impacts on Employee Welfare," *Industrial and Labor Relations Review* 53 (2000), no. 2: 179–196.

	1992	1997
Quality circles and/or off-line problem-solving groups	27.4	57.4
Job rotation	26.6	55.5
Self-managed work teams	40.5	38.4
Total Quality Management	24.5	57.2
Two or more practices	26.0	70.7
Three or more practices	14.2	39.5

How do these work systems affect the performance of firms and the welfare of employees? Although perfect experimental research like that often done in medicine (in which randomly selected firms adopt the systems and others do not) is obviously not possible, a large and growing body of field work within and across industries has now documented that the new work systems outperform traditional models, at least with respect to productivity and quality. Firm-specific and industry-specific studies have shown this to be true in automobiles,[29] steel,[30] telecommunications,[31] apparel,[32] trucking,[33] and office equipment.[34] More recently, national cross-sectional and panel studies have documented similar positive effects of workplace innovations on productivity, quality, and profitability

A considerable number of studies also find these new work systems to have salutary effects on job satisfaction and commitment, turnover, grievance rates, and labor-management relations.[35] Although the number of studies along these lines is still quite small and the results are not uniform, the best evidence suggests that encouraging the expansion of knowledge-based or high-performance work systems should have economic benefits for individual firms and for the overall economy. Whether employees share in the benefits of these innovations in terms of increased earnings and employment security, however, appears to depend on whether workers have an independent voice in these processes.[36]

Labor-Management Partnerships

In the unionized sector, one response to difficulties confronting firms as they adapt new business models has been innovative union-management partnerships. None of these partnerships are without problems, and some have proved disappointing. Nonetheless, they are worth highlighting, as they suggest responses that may be applicable not only to unionized firms but also to other enterprises that choose to pursue cooperation with their workers.

San Francisco Hotels

In 1993 a multi-employer group composed of ten of the largest unionized hotels in San Francisco proposed to the leaders of Local 2 of the Hotel Employees and Restaurant Employees Union that they try to change what had been a highly adversarial relationship and that they explore ways to work together more effectively. Out of these negotiations came an agreement to treat their relationship as a "living contract" according to which they would work together to address problems. In the first 5 years under this approach, the parties created a joint job training fund, agreed to open a pilot restaurant with lower base wages and more flexible job assignments, improved and expanded the hiring hall, and improved pension plans. In 1999 the parties renegotiated this agreement and extended it to 2004. In addition to agreeing to expand the concept of the pilot restaurant to five new sites and to continue to fund their joint training program, the parties added a provision for consultation on how to handle a number of immigration issues. The joint efforts under this collective bargaining relationship mirror the issues and interests that we foresee in future employment relationships. The parties are investing in training to enhance skills, productivity, and service quality, working with the work force and with immigration officials to address the complex issues facing the largely immigrant work force and their families, working together to meet the goals of overlapping government regulations and to integrate them with privately negotiated benefits and working conditions, and exploring new ways to organize work and to design and open new businesses that will create jobs and profits.

Labor-management conflicts have not disappeared in any of the partnerships discussed above, nor should we expect them to do so. Instead, using negotiation, employee participation, and labor-management partnerships, the parties have worked to improve how they address conflicts and problems in their relationship. These efforts alone cannot overcome unfavorable market developments, but they do represent efforts to better adapt labor-management relations to a changing economy and a changing work force.

Saturn

The Saturn Corporation is the most extensive example of the use of stakeholder principles to design and manage a firm. Saturn was conceived of as a full partnership between a union and a company. The decision to create Saturn was motivated by General Motors' and the United Auto Workers' desire to build and sell in the United States a small car that would compete well against imports and to create jobs for UAW members.

Saturn's organizational design makes the UAW an institutional "partner," participating in consensus-based decision making from the shop floor to the levels of senior management. This structure is overseen by a series of consultative and co-management structures at the department, plant or business-unit, manufacturing-policy, and strategic-policy levels of the organization. Through the partnership's arrangements, the UAW is an important part of strategic decisions made regarding supplier and retailer selection, choice of technology, and product development. Front line workers are also organized into work teams and management responsibilities are shared between union and company representatives at all levels from first line supervision to the top of the management structure.

Saturn has been well received in the marketplace, achieving among the highest customer satisfaction ratings of any car built in America between 1992 and 1997. Its productivity and profitability, however, are not as high as its quality ratings.

Despite its successes, Saturn is a controversial topic within both the UAW International Union and GM. Several years after Saturn was created, its original champions within both the UAW and GM retired. Their successors were not as committed to Saturn's principles and partnership structure. In the late 1990s, UAW leadership and the leaders of the Saturn local experienced considerable internal conflict over a host of issues, ranging from the adequacy of representation on traditional issues to shift schedules, overtime and shift premiums, and other administrative matters. Political factions arose within the local (similar to the dynamics at other UAW local unions).

GM management has also been ambivalent about Saturn. On the one hand, the corporation relishes the positive image that Saturn has achieved; on the other hand, it has not extended the labor-management partnership principles to any of its other divisions. Moreover, in 1996 GM decided to accede to UAW International's preference to build the second-generation Saturn model in Wilmington, Delaware, rather than in Spring Hill,

Tennessee, as requested by the local union and management. Only after being pressured by the local union in contract negotiations in 1998 did GM agree to source a second-generation product (a sport-utility vehicle) in Spring Hill, but only 5 years after the company's original plan called for introduction of a second-generation model.

Saturn represents not only the most comprehensive labor-management partnership model found in the United States but also an organization that embodies many of the principles of what is meant by a "stakeholder" corporation Saturn was designed to achieve both GM's shareholders' goal of making a small car profitably and the work force's and the union's goal of building small cars in the United States with American workers and UAW members. This fact implies that the success of the firm should be measured against these multiple objectives. Whether Saturn's limited profitability to date implies that this organizational model inevitably redistributes some of the financial rewards across the different stakeholders at the expense of shareholders is still an open question—one that is likely to be the subject of considerable debate in the future. Thus, despite the positive publicity that the UAW-Saturn partnership has received and its success on the quality and marketing fronts, the ambivalent support from both parents (UAW International and GM), leave the future of Saturn somewhat uncertain.

Xerox

Xerox has a long-standing employee-involvement program and a long-standing labor-management partnership with the union that represents its hourly workers, the United Needletrades, Industrial, and Textile Employees (UNITE).[37] The employee-involvement process began in 1980 after the parties included an agreement to experiment with this process in their collective bargaining agreement. The parties also agreed that Xerox executives would meet twice a year to share information about the current and future state of the business with top union leaders. But Xerox and the union confronted the conflict between job security and their continued efforts to implement employee involvement as early as 1982. The company was under pressure to outsource labor-intensive work such as the manufacture and assembly of wire harnesses, yet the union and the company had an active employee-involvement process underway with this group of workers. The solution was to establish a study team to see if the work could be done competitively in house. The study team recommended a broad array of changes in the organization of work, in the movement and assignment of personnel, in the roles and the numbers of supervisors, in accounting systems, in plant layout and work scheduling, and in other production systems. These changes reduced the cost of doing this work by more than $3 million per year and thereby closed the cost differential available from outside vendors. This type of jointly agreed-to flexibility then led to the negotiation of successive job-security guarantees in collective bargaining that have sustained and expanded the workplace innovations at Xerox for 20 years.

Five successor collective bargaining agreements have been negotiated since 1980, the most recent for a long-term contract lasting from 1994 to 2001. That agreement proved to be controversial both within the company and the union. It provided for a set of new, lower-wage classifications for several entry-level positions and for the flexibility to hire more temporary workers, but in return it provided for the continuation of guaranteed employment security for incumbent workers through 2001. Amidst these negotiations were rumors that some management officials were exploring the option of moving much or all of the company's manufacturing operations from Rochester to North Carolina and other operations to Mexico. The company's decision to negotiate a long-term agreement signaled the defeat of

the North Carolina option and a commitment to maintain operations in Rochester, at least for the duration of the contract.

The Xerox-UNITE partnership is the most enduring example
of the strengths and potential of sustained innovation and adap-
tation in American labor-management relations. It also demonstrates such a partnership's vulnerability to the pressures that
companies and workers now face due to changing technologies
and market uncertainties. Finally, it provides a glimpse of what it
takes to respond to these challenges. It is grounded in a proven
shop-floor participative process. Quantitative and case-study
research validated the contributions of these processes.[38] It integrated the collective bargaining process into the change effort—
using bargaining to join tough job security issues in 1983 and
again in 1994 but also conducting negotiations in a fashion that
reinforced the values and substantive objectives of the shop-floor
participation and the organizational transformation process. The
process has been supported and reinforced by the strong commitment of CEOs and of union officials, and this commitment
has been passed down through successive leadership transitions.

Two limitations of this strategy should be noted. One relates
to the risks that manufacturing employees at Xerox, like their
counterparts elsewhere, face. The second relates to the fact that
coverage of the partnership is limited to 4000 hourly manufacturing employees out of the 90,000 workers employed in the
United States by Xerox. The manufacturing work force is likely
to shrink in size, regardless of whether work is outsourced or
performed within Xerox. Through joint agreement, the fact that
job growth at Xerox lies outside the bargaining unit has been
kept off the table and off limits for the union. How the service
technicians and sales representatives and the supervisory and
middle managers at Xerox will fare as the same pressures of technological change and uncertainty in the marketplace play out is
a big question for the company and its employees. In addition,

the lines dividing these groups from those in the bargaining unit are becoming increasingly blurred. Yet these groups have no voice in the partnership, and they were not protected by the employment security agreements. Although a variety of other informal groups and processes are used to involve non-represented technical and managerial employees, they are not covered by the job security features of the union contract. Engaging them in an effort to update their social contracts is a challenge facing not just Xerox but American society in general.

The New Economy Revisited: The Case of the Biotechnology Industry

Before we summarize the lessons that are to be drawn from the cases discussed above, a brief look at employment practices and issues in another prototypical "new economy" industry is in order. Let us consider the biotechnology industry in Massachusetts, drawing on research done by Susan Eaton and her colleagues at the Radcliffe Public Policy Institute.[39]

What are the central employment issues facing these firms and workers? Some are no different than the challenges of their older industry counterparts. Because only one in ten of these firms survive, job security is a critical issue. But because everyone knows that the risk of job loss or firm failure is high, few expect individual firms to provide job security. Instead, employees expect these firms to provide opportunities to learn so that they will have the skills and experience that allow them to find their next job if and when this becomes necessary. Employees also value positive relations with co-workers highly, both because they expect to learn from them and to work closely with them on project teams and because they need to build enduring social ties and networks to help one another find jobs in the future. Finally, perhaps because nearly half of the work force is female and the work force is relatively young, work/family issues play a central role in employment relations. Family-friendly benefits and flexibility in work hours are widespread in the industry. But here, as in other settings, the use of these benefits is consistently lower than one might expect in view of their availability. The best predictors of their use and of their contributions to work and life satisfaction are whether employees feel free to use them without fearing negative consequences for their careers and the degree of control employees have over their use.

This case, then, provides a glimpse at the types of institutions that will be needed to support working in "new economy" firms and industries. Job security will come more through institutions that support mobility than from long tenure in a single firm. Networking and lifelong learning to keep skills current will be critical to reducing the costs of mobility. Employees will value institutions that support positive workplace cultures that promote learning and positive social interactions and that allow employees to control use of their time without fear of reprisal or negative career consequences.

Conclusion

There is enormous variation in the nature of organizational forms and employment relationships today. Large firms are not going away, nor are small firms. However, the boundaries of firms of all sizes are less stable, and therefore what work will be done (and who will do it) in house or elsewhere in the value chain is more uncertain than in the past. This makes it more difficult for individual firms to carry out and provide some of the labor-market functions and services that society has come to expect of them. It also makes it more difficult for firm-based collective bargaining or labor-management partnerships to function in a stable and sustained fashion. If (as we expect in view of the forces of globalization and changing technologies) these uncertainties continue, more of these labor-market functions will fall to the external labor market and to institutions that support the movement of workers across firms and that coordinate cross-firm interactions.

Yet we are not moving to a completely fluid labor market and to completely fluid careers for all workers. A large number of workers will continue to be employed in the same organization for long periods of time. Recall from the data presented in chapter 2 that tenure has declined but the median tenure still is about 5 years for workers in the age range 35–44 and 10 years for those in the age range 55–64. Indeed, a significant number of firms are engaged in efforts to transform their practices in ways that draw more fully on employees' knowledge and skills. Those efforts in which employees have an independent voice in shaping decisions appear to be able to serve both shareholder and employee interests. Thus, the need for voice within the firm remains important. Labor-management partnerships have proved useful in providing workers a voice in the key decisions affecting their jobs; however, they are limited in number and in the percentage of workers within an enterprise they cover, and they are hard to sustain when organizational boundaries are unstable. Workplace participation processes, when embedded in more comprehensive knowledge-driven or high-performance work systems, improve performance and build human capital, but by law and practice they are limited as instruments for addressing the full array of workers' and employers' concerns.

Within many firms, particularly those emerging in the "new economy," there is a new dividing line separating employees who are in high demand because their knowledge and skills are important to the core activities or strategies of the firm from employees who perform routine or support services and/or who are more at risk of having their function outsourced. Because knowledge has become a central asset and labor markets are highly competitive, newer, rapidly growing firms are going to great lengths to attract and retain these individuals, including offering an array of "family-friendly" benefits and services. But few of these benefits are extended to lower-level workers performing services outside what are deemed to be the "core competencies" of the firm. These workers live with the risk of having their jobs outsourced to specialized contractors.

But, as the case of Southwest Airlines, studies in banking and telecommunications, and the evidence beginning to accumulate from studies of new startups suggest, human resources may be indeed be a potential source of competitive advantage, customer satisfaction, and positive employment outcomes for those firms that choose to organize and compete in this fashion. If this is the case, then perhaps we are on the brink of inventing a new business and organizational model: the human-capital-based corporation. For years, human-resources professionals and business writers have called human resources "our most important asset" without being able to deliver the policies or the practices that sustain commitment to a "high-road" strategy. Yet the evidence from both manufacturing and services suggests that this is a possible (but alas not the only possible) way to compete. If this is true, then more efforts are needed to make this strategy more viable and more transparent to the corporate insiders who determine the basic strategies of the firm and to investors (who should be asking for information on these aspects of a firm's strategies and competencies).

All this leads to a conclusion that no single means for reconciling or integrating employees' and shareholders' interests is likely to suffice. Indeed, society has a strong interest in encouraging individual firms to adopt strategies that generate value from their full work force, not just their elite "knowledge" workers. Policies and institutions should be geared to encouraging and supporting these high-road business models and employment relationships.

But it is more and difficult for an individual firm to go it alone. Firms will have to be engaged in constructive relationships with external labor-market institutions. External institutions will likely take on greater roles, particularly in settings where technology continues to change where and how work is done.

Thus, efforts within individual companies to adapt practices and norms are necessary but not sufficient requirements for building a new social contract at work that fits current realities. We have identified the need for further institutional innovations to support such individual company-employee-union efforts. Efforts within these individual employment relationships must be supplemented by community, labor-market, and perhaps industry-level institutional innovations capable of overcoming the inherent limits of individual firms' efforts. These external institutions may be more important now than in the past, in view of the changing markets and technologies that limit the promises and commitments that an individual firm can make to its employees. What these external institutions should be, and how individual firms and unions should relate to or participate in them, will be taken up in chapters 4 and 5.

4

Extended Networks: A Vision for Next-Generation Unions

The previous chapter illustrated how it is becoming increasingly difficult for individual firms, working on their own or with unions through collective bargaining, to carry out many of the functions expected of them under the New Deal system of employment relations. But these functions are still very much needed by American workers. Job placement, training and development of human capital, monitoring and improving on employment standards, health insurance and retirement benefits, real wage growth, and voice or representation at work are as important and necessary for workers and their families in today's economy as they were in yesterday's. Historically, labor unions provided many of these functions through collective bargaining. In addition, unions have served a critical political and social role, giving workers a voice in community, state, and national governments.

Yet, as we documented in chapter 2, union membership and collective bargaining coverage have declined to the point where there is serious doubt as to whether unions can now, or in the future, serve these functions for American workers and society. As we noted in chapter 1, we continue to believe in the need for and the value of unions in society. So do 75 percent of the American public[1] and thoughtful leaders in the business community.[2] Workers and their families need and deserve a strong, independent, and innovative voice in the workplace, in their communities, and in national policy making. History tells us, however, that unions are successful only when they adapt to and match up well with the structure of the economy, with employers' organizational forms, and with the preferences and needs of the work force. In view of the significant changes in these features discussed in previous chapters, it is obvious that unions have a tall order in store.

In our view, the central challenge facing unions and other forms of employee voice is the heterogeneity of the American workplace. As a consequence of this diversity unions, and other representatives of employees, need to experiment with and adopt a range of organizational forms.[3] The effort to find what forms succeed in what circumstances is, we believe, both a considerable challenge and a considerable opportunity.

But more than just adapting to a variety of particular circumstances, unions must build scale and scope. Scale today requires new, more varied forms of organizing and coalition building, linking together not just different unions and employee organizations but also those community groups and organizations that advocate for workers' and human rights concerns independent of any workplace connection. Building scope in turn requires that unions appeal to the needs and interests of workers across a wide, if not the full, occupational spectrum. In view of the shift away from blue-collar manufacturing industries and toward white-collar service and high-tech industries, unions need to develop new organizing strategies aimed at technical, professional, and white-collar workers whose identities and interests often make them less receptive to the traditional appeals of unions. Likewise, in view of the demise of internal labor markets within large corporations and the increase in mobility across work sites, unions must develop ways of assisting workers with their job placement and training needs. Finally, since our system of employee representation has been rooted primarily in the enterprise and a clear division of labor within it, unions must struggle to launch representation strategies encompassing workers whose jobs do not fit neatly into the "non-exempt" category and who work outside of or across several different enterprises.

In this chapter we identify four segments of the labor market that we believe require distinctive approaches to enhancing employee voice: the industrial and craft sectors (in which unions have had long-term strength), professionals and managers, contingent workers, and employees trapped in low-income labor markets. For each of these segments we provide examples of innovative union strategies for addressing the distinctive needs of each segment. In addition to focusing on the diversity of the labor market, we emphasize the diversity of possible responses. While examining how established unions have responded or might respond to these challenges, we also report new forms of workers' organizations, some of which grow out of unions and some of which are emerging from less traditional sources (such as community groups and employee caucuses).

It may be useful to preview the vision of the "next-generation unions"[4] that will emerge from our analysis. Our experience tells us that if we don't do this up front, many readers will conjure up negative stereotypes that will blind them to the merits of the ideas presented here. Indeed, when presenting these ideas to different groups, we have seen "union," "next-generation union," or some alternative term that captures the functions we see for organizations that represent workers become lightening rods. On the one hand, people who have little or no contact with unions (and this is the vast majority of employees and managers today) see them as outdated relics of the old economy. They can't get past the union label to focus on what unions have done in the past, are struggling to do today, or need to do in the future. At a recent gathering of corporate work and family professionals, for example, one thoughtful participant put it this way: "I know that our efforts could be helped and our influence increased if employees had a stronger voice, but the term 'union' carries so many negative images with me and my management colleagues that I can't imagine how I could do my work successfully in a union environment."

At the other extreme, a number of unionists who have heard us discuss the ideas developed here about the need for multiple forms of representation have automatically interpreted our view as an argument for the "TEAM Act" (a proposal to eliminate bans on employee participation that union leaders see as likely to undermine "legitimate" and "independent" unions and collective bargaining). This is the case even though we oppose the TEAM Act for failing to include adequate protections for workers' rights and failing to address the full range of problems with existing labor law. We want to break out of both of these frames of reference.

We see the "next-generation unions" as coalition partners offering political voice, direct participation, collective bargaining, strategic partnerships, mobility, and occupational community. To adapt to the changing industrial structure and to the varied circumstances and needs of workers, we envision them as extended networks[5] that represent and serve workers' interests in a variety of ways inside firms, in local areas and labor markets, in professional communities, and in political affairs. They would use multiple methods and tools—grounded in collective bargaining, in workers' participation, and in broader labor-management partnerships, but supplemented by full use of modern communications technologies and personal networks—to provide information, education, technical advice, and assistance to individuals and groups, and to articulate and communicate workers' concerns and perspectives to the public and to political leaders. Like employers, they will need to be open organizations with fuzzy and porous boundaries between "unions" as they have been traditionally organized in industrial or craft jurisdictions and local, national, international, and federated structures and various coalition partners in the religious, non-governmental, government, educational, research, and even employer communities. Linking together unions and coalition partners at the community level in particular will take on significantly greater importance in the future than in the recent past. Individuals will need to be able to move across these boundaries shifting their "primary membership" from one to another at different stages of their careers and family lives. But once they join the extended network, they should be considered a member for life, just as an individual, once accepted by a college, becomes a member of that school's extended family for life. Whether we call these extended networks "unions" or something else is perhaps a matter we can leave to readers from different ideological traditions to decide for themselves.

With this in mind, let us briefly review what workers say they want and need from unions today. We will then illustrate some of the innovative efforts underway in existing unions and in other workers' advocacy groups and organizations. Finally, we will summarize how we envision these groups and organizations fitting together into an extended network.

What Employees Want

Do Americans still believe that unions are needed? An enormous body of survey evidence about workers' views of work and their expectations for a voice at work has been amassed. The consistent findings of studies dating from the 1970s to today are the following:

• Workers want a direct and influential voice in decisions affecting their work and employment conditions.
• A substantial number of unorganized workers want to address many of these issues through either unions or some other form of group or collective effort.
• There is an upward trend in both of these preferences since 1980.

In the 1970s a series of nationally representative surveys on the "Quality of Employment" were conducted for the US Department of Labor by the Survey Research Center at the University of Michigan. The 1977 study clearly documented that workers wanted more of a say in how to do their work, in what kinds of training opportunities were available to them, in how new technologies would affect their work, and on an array of "bread and butter" issues including wages, safety and health, and job security.[6] Other studies conducted in the early 1980s showed that workers' expectations exceeded the actual amount of say or influence they experienced on their jobs.[7] These basic findings applied to blue-collar and white-collar employees, to men, to women, to whites, and to people of color.

The predictive pattern of these factors has remained quite stable. What has changed is the percentage indicating a preference for joining a union. It has gone up. Recent surveys report numbers in the range of 43–47 percent and as high as 57 percent for young workers.[8] Thus, the constituency for a traditional union as envisioned in the eyes of non-union American workers when asked this type of question is larger today than it was in the past. However, it is still a minority of the work force. Since American labor law requires a majority of a specific unit or group of workers to vote to unionize before any worker gains representation, sole reliance on this core constituency will produce a labor movement composed of the most disenfranchised members of the labor force—those with few alternatives. Moreover, as long as unfair treatment is the primary motivator, who gets unionized is more in the hands of employers than it is in the hands of unions.

Recent surveys have also probed more deeply into the forms of representation and participation workers prefer and thus have documented significant variation in these preferences. A substantial number continue to prefer joining a union as traditionally envisioned, but nearly twice as many are asking for forms of representation that somehow combine the more informal participative and cooperative features often associated with various employee-involvement programs with the independent voice offered by unions. Unfortunately for those who express a preference for this approach, neither American labor law nor present management or labor ideologies encourage such an institutional arrangement. This was one of the key findings of the Worker Representation and Participation Survey, conducted by Richard Freeman of Harvard University and Joel Rogers of the University of Wisconsin. This survey, conducted in 1994, entailed a set of focus groups with workers in similar occupations, a half-hour national telephone survey of more than 2400 workers, and a follow-up mail-and-telephone survey of about 800 of the original respondents.

Like earlier surveys, the Worker Representation and Participation Survey showed that the vast majority of employees want more involvement and greater voice in company decisions affecting their workplace. For example, nearly two-thirds of the workers responded that they wanted more influence, whereas 35 percent were content to keep things as they were and 1 percent desired less influence.[9] On average the workers who wanted more influence were better educated and had longer tenure than the other workers, but the differences were minimal. Whether the respondents were divided into men vs. women, blacks vs.

whites, or high school graduates vs. college graduates, the results were the same: employees want a say in workplace decisions that affect them. The real differences have to do not with what workers want but with what they currently have. Workers with less education, workers with lower earnings, women, and blacks expressed having less influence at work than workers in stronger positions expressed. Unionized workers reported somewhat less influence than non-unionized workers. Participants in employee-involvement committees reported considerably more voice at work than non-participants.[10]

Asked why they wanted greater voice at the workplace, 87 percent of the respondents to the WRPS claimed that they would enjoy their jobs more if they were involved in decisions regarding production and operations; 75 percent believed that their firms would be more competitive as a result of this increased influence; 79 percent said that the quality of products and services would improve if employees had more say in decisions affecting production and operations. The majority of workers also reported that workplace conflicts would be more easily resolved if workers had greater voice at work. Interestingly enough, 58 percent of managers surveyed in the WRPS agreed with these workers, responding that workplace problems would be more effectively solved at their firm if employees collectively had more say.

In short, American workers want more say at the workplace. They want more say because they believe that it will improve the quality of their lives and because they think that it will make their companies more competitive.

But how should this voice and participation be expressed? On some issues, including harassment and training, workers surveyed in the WRPS preferred to express themselves as individuals. But on others, including workplace health and safety, pay, and benefits, workers preferred to speak as a group. Moreover, workers wanted cooperative relations with management. Though about one-third of all employees surveyed in the WRPS reported that management mistreated employees and was not trustworthy, few workers believed that the solution to these problems was institutionalized labor-management conflict. Instead, the vast majority believed that the more effective workplace organization is one that is independent but that also enjoys management participation and support. Finally, the vast majority of workers reported management resistance as the primary reason they did not have their desired level of influence at the workplace.

Similar results were reported from a March 1999 survey commissioned by the American Federation of Labor and Congress of Industrial Organizations (AFL-CIO). When asked how they would vote if an election were held tomorrow to decide whether your workplace would have a union or not," 43 percent of the respondents reported that they would either definitely or probably vote for forming a union, and 79 percent reported that they would probably or definitely vote to form an employee association. Again, employees believed that unions and other forms of collective representation would not only enhance their salaries and benefits but also provide them with voice on the job.[11] Thus, American workers have strong preferences for representation and participation, but widely varying views as to what forms would best suit their situation and their needs.

Responding to the New Labor Market

The most pressing challenge confronting unions is to find successful approaches to representing employees in the diverse settings in which they find themselves. The labor movement has in recent years engaged in a series of organizational and strategic innovations that have sought to rekindle its vitality and re-connect with workers, employers, and local communities. In 1995, John Sweeney, president of the Service Employees International Union, won the first contested election for president of the AFL-CIO. Sweeney and his slate ran on a platform of organizational reform and a radical reorientation toward new organizing. One of his first policy initiatives upon taking office was to announce that the AFL-CIO would allocate 30 percent of its resources to organizing—an unprecedented amount of money in view of the fact that in the past organizing was viewed as primarily the responsibility of the separate national unions, not the federation. Sweeney also urged individual unions to make similar allocations of their resources to organizing, and many did so. And Sweeney and his leadership team took other significant actions to renew the labor movement and to focus on organizing. An Organizing Institute was created to train staff in how to undertake this difficult process. In an effort to build support among college students, a Union Summer program was initiated to provide students with opportunities to learn about and try their hands at organizing workers. A Union Cities initiative was introduced to rejuvenate central labor councils in recognition of the increased importance of the community as an arena for coalition building, political activism, and union organizing. A unit was created to explore how unions should address issues of corporate strategy and governance and to foster workplace democracy.

We believe that these initiatives are important. At the same time, we are encouraged by efforts outside of the traditional union movement, including efforts by community organizations and efforts by affinity groups within firms, to find new ways to represent employees. In the remainder of this chapter we will describe innovations by unions and other groups to respond to the various needs of the new economy. As mentioned above, we will examine experiments and innovations in what we regard as the four main sectors of the labor market: unionized (industrial and craft) workers, contingent workers, professionals and managers, and low-income laborers.

Innovating in the Core

We start by examining the efforts of the Communications Workers of America, a union that is in many ways a prototype of the industrial unions that grew out of and prospered in the old economy under the auspices of the New Deal labor legislation but have been severely threatened by a changing competitive environment and by technology. The CWA, formed in the 1940s by the merger of a number of older company and regional telephone unions, gradually developed a more centralized structure. It began to engage in national bargaining with its dominant employer, AT&T, in 1970. However, after 1984 (when AT&T was forced to begin divesting its regional phone operations) bargaining in the communications industry gradually became more decentralized. Then, as new entrants into traditional telephone markets (e.g., Sprint and MCI) took market share from AT&T, and later as cable TV and the wireless and Internet portions of telecommunications grew, union membership plummeted.

Since the breakup of the Bell System, the CWA has been struggling to adapt to the changes underway in the industry while protecting its traditional base. The union's traditional core included blue-collar craft and service workers in the regulated telephone companies. With deregulation and technological innovation, the industry has changed to include not only new, non-union wireline companies but also wireless, cable, and TV firms. Moreover, the changing boundaries of the industry have led to a proliferation of new occupational groups employed within it. In addition to traditional occupational groups, such as network technicians, repairmen, splicers, and customer service workers, new kinds of workers such as computer programmers are now employed in the broader information-services industry. As a result of these changes in the contours of the industry and in the composition of its work force, the CWA has struggled to transform itself from a "telephone union" into the "union of the information age."[12]

This transformation has created several challenges for the union. The first challenge concerns the size of the labor force. Before the divestiture of AT&T, roughly a million people were employed in the telephone industry. Today more than 6 million work in the broader information-services sector. Thus, although the CWA's membership of 650,000 is more or less what it was in the early 1980s, union density in this sector has fallen from approximately 67 percent in 1982 to 27 percent in 1997.[13] Even within AT&T, union membership had fallen from more than 200,000 to approximately 40,000 by 1999—from essentially 100 percent of the non-exempt labor force to about 50 percent. Second, as described above, many of the new workers in the industry are quite occupationally different from the union's traditional base of craft and service workers. Yet, perhaps more important, a significant number are employed in non-standard work arrangements —for example, as independent contractors, temporary workers, and freelancers. Thus, the CWA has had to develop new campaigns to address the varied employment situations and occupational concerns of this new work force. Finally, not only the workers but also the employers have changed in this industry. Before the breakup, the CWA had a long-standing relationship with a handful of companies and bargained a national collective agreement across the entire Bell System. Today the union faces not only the reconfigured and downsized Regional Bell Operating Companies (Verizon, Bell South, Ameritech, etc.) but also myriad other small and large firms in other segments of the industry that are non-union and/or anti-union.

The CWA has responded to these challenges in a variety of ways, including using collective bargaining and using its influence with government regulatory boards to extract neutrality agreements with the traditional Regional Bell Operating Companies (RBOCs). In 1989, for example, the CWA successfully negotiated agreements with each of the RBOCs and with AT&T that provided for management neutrality in organizing drives and either card check recognition or elections that would be governed by specific rules designed to expedite the process and avoid negative attacks on the company or the union by one party or the other. Although the implementation of these agreements has not been entirely smooth (both the union and the companies have argued that negative campaigning and other practices that violate the agreed-upon norms and procedures continue to occur), the agreements are beginning to pay off in union growth. This example demonstrates the pivotal role of management resistance or neutrality in determining the ability of private-sector unions to organize successfully.

In contrast with the small successes at AT&T and in the RBOCs, the CWA has not been able to penetrate the newer non-union companies either in the core telephone line of business, or in the newer wireless, cable, and Internet segments of the industry. These companies have vigorously fought union organizing efforts. The case of Sprint in San Francisco is a classic example. After more than 5 years of legal battling over whether or not the union won recognition rights through an election, a US Court of Appeals overturned a National Labor Relations Board ruling that had granted the employees recognition in light of what it judged to be a decision by Sprint to close this branch operation after a successful organizing campaign.

The CWA also provides associational membership to individual workers employed in non-union enterprises or in non-standard employment arrangements. The best-known example is the Washington Alliance of Technology Workers ("WashTech"), an organization of software professionals at Microsoft and other high-tech companies who are affiliated with the CWA through the Newspaper Guild.

In an effort to build a presence outside of its traditional wire-line telephone base, the CWA has merged with a variety of unions representing workers in the broader information-services indus-try. In 1987 it merged with the International Typographical Union, in 1994 with the National Association of Broadcast Employees and Technicians (NABET), and in 1995 with the Newspaper Guild. In 1998 some 2500 workers at Dow Jones joined the CWA, and in 2000 some 40,000 members of the International Electrical Workers joined the CWA. In addition to boosting membership, these mergers have strengthened the union's presence in the content side of the information industry and among white-collar technical and professional employees. For example, NABET includes engineers, news writers, announc-ers, and directors who work for ABC, NBC, and more than 100 private radio, TV, and film companies. The Newspaper Guild represents journalists, photographers, translators, and inter-preters, and on-line writers and designers. These new members have facilitated the CWA's efforts to reach out to unorganized white-collar and professional workers in the new (and growing) sectors of the industry. As a result of these successes, the CWA is now exploring mergers with the American Federation of Musicians, Theatrical and Stage Workers and with other unions.

Thus, CWA is an industrial union that is attempting to adapt to the reconfiguration of its industry—an industry with an expanded array of older unionized firms and newer non-unionized competitors operating in traditional and new busi-nesses. The union has used collective bargaining to negotiate limits on employers' opposition to new union organizing wher-ever it could, and these agreements have begun to produce some union growth. It has attempted to organize other more tradi-tionally anti-union employers with traditional approaches through the NLRB election process, but it has not been able to overcome the resistance of those employers. It has experimented with selected use of association membership strategies outside collective bargaining, and it has attracted small numbers of new members through these approaches. And it has stabilized and broadened the base of its membership by absorbing and by merging with smaller unions representing various technical and professional occupations. Despite this range of strategies, the vast majority of workers in the telecommunications and information-services industries are not represented today.

In many ways, construction unions have represented the stereotypical (negative) image of American unionism. They were seen, and at times they behaved, as highly exclusive, bureaucratic, and conservative. Where these unions were strong, they controlled access to high-wage work. Entry into the unions and their apprenticeship jobs was difficult. Often, women and minority workers were excluded. Today, however, construction trade unions are among the most innovative organizations in the American labor movement. Having suffered dramatic losses in membership and influence in an industry that has experienced a significant increase in employment growth in recent years, the various construction trade unions have embarked on a series of experiments that are redefining their relations with employers, with non-union workers, and even with their members.

From a high of 80 percent union density in the 1940s, construction unions today represent less than 20 percent of the work force in the industry. The decline in membership has been steep. The carpenters' and the painters' unions have lost more than half of their membership. Membership in the construction trades overall has declined by one-third. Residential construction is almost completely non-union, light commercial construction (i.e., construction of small office buildings and apartment complexes) is largely non-union.

In response to this dramatic decline in influence and membership, building-trades unions have engaged in organizational and strategic reforms aimed at revitalizing their structures and regaining centrality in the industry. These reforms include creating innovative strategies for organizing workers, forging new relationships with contractors and owners, revitalizing their training and apprenticeship programs, and making significant structural changes within the unions. For example, in recent years several of the unions have launched initiatives in training and skill formation. Training and apprenticeship programs have traditionally been among the most important of the construction trade unions' tools for recruiting new workers and defending themselves against assaults by non-union (open-shop) employers. Despite efforts by open-shop employers to usurp their position, the trade unions maintain clear dominance over the training of the most highly skilled workers in the market. Through their worst days of the 1980s, all the trade unions ensured that their training and apprenticeship programs remained strong. Advocates of the open shop admit that it does a poor job of developing and funding training programs for skilled workers in the industry.[14]

Further ensuring that it will remain in the forefront of training, the International Brotherhood of Electrical Workers has invested heavily in electronic media that will supplement its comprehensive fixed site training programs. In addition, the IBEW is establishing relationships with colleges to offer college-level credit for the highly technical training that electricians receive. The IBEW has also created two new sub-journeyman categories. Workers can now choose to enter a 2-year Residential Electrical Technician apprenticeship or a 2–3-year Telecommunication Technician program instead of pursuing the traditional five-year Journeyman Master Electrician program. The carpenters' unions, too, have created specialty programs, including one in asbestos removal.

Moreover, the carpenters' unions have embarked on an ambitious advertising campaign emphasizing union members' high levels of training, skills, pride, and quality of work. These efforts are designed to capture new and emerging markets and bring them under unions' control. By ensuring that they are on top of emerging areas within their markets, unions are not only securing their place in the center of the market for these skills but also keeping the open shop from making further inroads.

Organizing Professionals and Managers

In 1997 the Committee of Interns and Residents (CIR), which represents 9000 medical interns and residents in six states, affiliated with the Service Employees International Union. The CIR joined with other physicians' unions to form the National Doctors' Alliance, which bargains collectively for 15,000 doctors. The CIR thus serves as an example of how professional workers and their associations are evolving toward collective bargaining.

As physicians have felt increasing pressure from health-maintenance organizations and from insurance companies, unions have grown more appealing to them. The organizing of interns and residents seems less unusual, in view of their limited control over their work and their working conditions. According to Sandra Shea of the CIR: "Many of their concerns are basic trade union issues like making a living wage to put food on the table and to pay back enormous student loans, dealing with unusually long working hours and poor working conditions. They walk a fine line between the really hard work it takes to learn this profession and outright exploitation and misuse of their time and concern for humanity."

Most unionized interns and residents are found in the public sector, where public labor boards tend to grant them the status of employee. In the private sector, where the majority of interns and residents work, a ruling by the NLRB denied these same young doctors that same status, labeling them students. However, the CIR got this decision overturned by bringing a case against the Boston Medical Center. With this victory, the CIR will be able to engage in collective bargaining for significantly larger numbers of people.

At the same time, the CIR has been busy handling physicians' growing interest in unions. According to Sandra Shea: "The phone is ringing off the hook at the National Doctors' Alliance in response to our post-residency physician organizing campaign. Many have an interest in unionizing because they've lost control of their professions. They're angry with the American Medical Association for looking the other way." In fact, a contentious internal debate is raging within the American Medical Association over whether it should establish a collective bargaining arm similar to that created by the American Nursing Association. Regardless of which umbrella organization physicians choose to organize under, this previously untapped segment of the labor market may serve to infuse new energy (not to mention new people) into the American labor movement. There are approximately 600,000 post-residency doctors in the United States, and the estimate is that almost 40 percent already fall into what would be considered an "employee" category. In fact, doctors' unions are sprouting up in New York, in Washington, in Arizona, and elsewhere. This development, along with similar ones among engineers, professional psychologists, and software professionals, promises to reshape not only various professional labor markets and industries but also the American union movement as more and more professional workers enter its ranks.

In the United States and elsewhere, a number of unions are experimenting with new ways to recruit and meet the professional needs of their members. An initiative by the American Federation of Teachers to recruit and provide representational and other professional services to psychologists (many of whom are independent contractors) recognizes that many professionals, in the course of their careers, will move in and out of different types of employment arrangements, sometimes being classified as independent contractors or consultants, sometimes working part time for multiple employers, and sometimes perhaps employed full time by a single clearly defined employer. The task of organizations that want to represent these types of workers is to stay with them through these changes in their employment status.

The National Education Association sees its task as one of representing professionals for "employability" rather than for "employment security" in any single job they might hold at a particular point in time. A big part of the NEA's strategy involves creative use of the Web, CD-ROMs, and related technologies to provide professional services to current and future members. A few examples: Each new member receives a CD-ROM containing information about member services, updated information on professional development opportunities, etc. Several "virtual conferences" for new members have been held in which new members can watch or listen to speeches by people such as the "teacher of the year," can interact with one another and with NEA staff in "hallway discussions" or other focused sessions. A customized personal Web page is under development in which each new member can receive information tailored to his or her specific needs.

A professional union in another part of the world that is using cyberspace and other services to recruit and serve its members is the Association of Professional Engineers, Scientists, and Managers of Australia (APESMA). This association represents a mix of professionals in various occupations, both through collective negotiations and through a variety of membership services. Among other things, it takes a "full career life cycle" approach by offering university students free affiliate membership, career advice, and placement assistance. When these students graduate and enter their professional careers, APESMA offers a distance-learning MBA program in technology management; a front-line management diploma educational program; placement and recruitment of engineering, management, and technical employees; salary and benefit surveys for different occupations; legal services; negotiation of collective agreements; assistance in negotiating individual employment contracts; accountancy services; retirement benefits plan; and group discounts for Internet access, travel, medical and hospital insurance, credit cards, and financial services.

Organizing In Low-Income Labor Markets

One of the truly fascinating examples of union innovation is the Service Employees International Union's successful campaign to organize new kinds of workers at both the top and the bottom of the labor market.

The case of home-care workers typifies the difficulties that unions encounter in organizing low-wage workers today. In addition to being poorly paid, many are minorities and/or immigrants, a majority are mothers, and all are employed in the homes of their clients. The story of the SEIU's success in organizing 75,000 home-care workers in Los Angeles County illustrates the importance of forging lasting coalitions between the union movement and other organizations in the local community and the importance of constructing new institutions to govern work and employment relations in the new economy.

Home-care programs came into being in the 1970s as social services designed to assist elderly and disabled individuals in daily activities, including cleaning, cooking, and bathing. By living at home instead of in a nursing home or some other institution, clients could maintain their independence and their connections to their communities.[15] Many home-care programs came about as the result of lobbying efforts on the part of the emerging senior citizen and disability lobbies.[16]

The state of California apportioned a pool of money for home-care services and devolved the administration of the program to the counties. Every county set up its own In-Home Supportive Service system (IHSS) through its social service agencies. The California Supreme Court ruled that neither the county (which created eligibility standards for consumers and decided how many hours and what services consumers received) nor the state (which issued the workers' checks) was the employer. The clients, the court ruled, were the employers. Thus, home-care workers had no entity with which they could collectively bargain. To reverse this ruling, the SEIU turned to the state legislature, which in 1992 passed a law giving the counties a new option for how to deliver services: A county could create a public authority that would serve as the employer of record, particularly for purposes of collective bargaining if the home-care workers voted to be represented by a union.

Although Los Angeles County initially resisted the establishment of a centralized public authority governed by a board of supervisors, the SEIU, in collaboration with an array of disability and senior citizen groups, was able to pressure the county to establish one in 1992. The SEIU then set out to organize the 75,000 home-care workers in the county. Union organizers knocked on the doors of 30,000 workers, of whom 10,600 signed cards to join the local and to petition the new public authority to hold an election. The SEIU brought in 75 additional organizers from other locals and from other parts of the United States, and Local 434B employed 22 full-time organizers in the last year of the recognition campaign. In February 1999 the election was held. Ballots were distributed in English, Spanish, and Armenian. Approximately 25 percent of the ballots were returned, and the result was a victory for the union. Negotiations are now underway between the union and the public authority to establish a registry, create training programs, raise wages, and provide health benefits, all of which will be funded by the state.

Organizing these workers required considerable use of political power at the state and local levels of government; it also required an organizing strategy capable of reaching and communicating with a multi-cultural labor force in the workers' homes, in churches, in community centers, and elsewhere, rather than in their workplaces. Similar efforts will be needed to reach and attract other low-wage workers.

Increasingly, community groups are organizing around issues of work and economic development and are offering representation, training, and organizing assistance to low-income and immigrant workers across employers and industries. Some of these efforts are done in coalition with unions, but some community groups form and operate on their own. These groups organize across territorial and industrial communities and take into account the diversity of workers' identities and interests. Their collective activity has led to what Janice Fine calls "community unionism."[17]

Examples of community organizing around labor-market issues are proliferating. National organizations such as the Industrial Areas Foundation and ACORN have partnered with local community groups to mount living-wage campaigns across the United States. On Long Island, the Workplace Project's immigrant workers' center induced the state legislature to pass a statewide unpaid-wages law. Baltimoreans United in Leadership Development (BUILD) has worked for the enactment of a series of city-wide labor-market ordinances (including living-wage, right-to-organize, and right-of-first refusal ordinances) and for a law that allows mothers moving off welfare to count education toward their work requirement.

Organizing Contingent Employees

As we noted in chapter 2, one of the characteristics of the new labor market is the increased use of contingent employees. These workers are in need of representation, but they are hard to organize because they are scattered among many work sites and because their employment tenures are so short. Nonetheless, there are a number of innovative efforts underway to reach and represent them.

One strategy rests on revitalizing the Central Labor Councils (CLCs). Historically these institutions engaged primarily in regional political and legislative action through electoral politics, fund raising, and lobbying. They also coordinated unions' responses to and their participation in a variety of community activities. Over the years, however, many of these structures atrophied, and thus their ability to engage effectively in political action, let alone coordinate local labor strategy, declined.

One of the first actions taken by John Sweeney as president of the AFL-CIO was to assemble leaders of the Central Labor Councils and discuss ways of revitalizing these bodies. The result of this meeting was a reorganization of the AFL-CIO's structures: four new regions were created, and new regional, state, and local directors were appointed. The new officers, in partnership with the Central Labor Council Advisory Committee (made up of a cross-section of CLC leaders), launched the Union Cities campaign, the idea behind which was to create stronger ties between local unions and community-based groups in an effort to improve working conditions at the local level. In many cities, CLCs have developed rapid response mechanisms for supporting organizing, contract battles, and community campaigns. CLCs continue their political work but have begun to refocus on building coalitions with local religious and community groups and on developing regional training programs aimed at promotion regional economic development. Through these new strategies, the CLCs hope to build greater union strength.

Perhaps one of the most exciting examples of a revitalized CLC is the South Bay Central Labor Council in San Jose, California. Located in the heart of Silicon Valley (considered a harbinger of the economy of the future), the South Bay Labor Council created a number of non-profit organizations aimed at rebuilding its own capacity and organizing workers in the new, traditionally unorganized information economy. For example, in 1995, the South Bay Labor Council, in partnership with various local organizations, created Working Partnerships, an organization seeking to promote local economic development and enhance union strength. One of the partnership's programs, called Together@Work, is an initiative aimed at making systematic changes in the region's temporary-employment industry. A membership-based organization that provides pension and health benefits and financial services, this labor-led temporary-employment agency meets regional skill standards set by an employer advisory committee The ultimate goal of this agency is to increase the wage floor for lower-paid "temp" work, and to help ensure greater employment stability for its workers. It seeks to position itself so as to be valued by local employers by supplying them with a stable supply of well-trained employees, and so as to be valued by workers by linking them to jobs, benefits, skill development, and social supports. In its early stages, Together@Work began to shift the terms of temporary employment in the region by becoming a competitive alternative to for-profit "temp" agencies. Amy Dean, president of the South Bay Labor Council, stated: "We're paying our temps $10 per hour—which isn't the final goal for wage levels—but we also provide benefits. Our competitors only pay $6 or $7 per hour without benefits at a higher cost to employers. With this strategy, we believe we can elevate the wage floor in this sector."[18] A similar effort, with similar goals, has recently been created in New Jersey by the Bergen County Labor Council.

Another innovative organization is Working Today, a national organization, based in New York, that has been promoting the concerns of self-employed workers since its founding in 1995. Founded by Sara Horowitz, Working Today has about 93,000 members. Its membership includes both individual members and associations (including the Newspaper Guild, the Translators and Interpreters Guild, and the New York Foundation for the Arts). Members pay annual dues of $25. In return they get access to group-rate health insurance, pre-paid legal advice, and a variety of discounts for travel, Internet access, computer purchases, and car rentals. Working Today operates a Web site and publishes a newsletter that informs members of its expanding services and of recent developments in laws and programs. It is now developing a Portable Benefits Fund intended to provide health insurance and pensions to the millions of workers who do not work full time for a single enterprise but rather work for several employers on a contingent and flexible basis. Drawing on the experiences of guilds, mutual-aid societies, and the American Association of Retired Persons, Working Today seeks to provide services and a collective voice. According to Horowitz, "the strategies of mutual aid and self-help groups were traditionally to pool benefits and resources, essentially to use capital to achieve certain goals while enabling the institutions that was created to participate in the democratic process."[19] Today there is a paucity of such organizations, and Working Today, through its own efforts and in collaboration with a network of other institutions and groups, hopes to build new ones.

Other Instruments for Employee Voice

In chapter 3 we noted that many workplaces in America now have some form of employee participation in place. Although the arrangements vary considerably in influence and in effectiveness, on average the data presented earlier in this chapter indicate that the majority of employees like them and want to see them grow in number and in influence. Informal participation processes are not substitutes for independent representation, and they are restricted by law from being used to negotiate wages or other terms and conditions of employment; however, some employers use them in their efforts to avoid unionization, and the evidence suggests that they are quite useful for that purpose.[20] The challenge for unions is to figure out how to turn these arrangements from competitors to complements of other forms of representation that the unions provide. Some unions are taking steps to do this. The International Association of Machinists and Aerospace Workers, for example, has a "High Performance Work Organization Partnerships Department" that works with its locals and with companies to implement workplace innovations consistent with the principles endorsed by the union.

The AFL-CIO's Center for Workplace Democracy is charged with promoting and providing technical assistance to affiliates seeking to implement workplace-democracy programs and/or labor-management partnerships within and across employers. A recent report cites more than 20 partnerships that link multiple employers and unions together to address workplace problems that would be difficult for any single organization to address on its own.[21] (An impressive example involving hotels in San Francisco was described in chapter 3.) Other groups have been organizing employees across firms, in local communities, within occupations, and according to certain social identities.

Where groups of individuals in the workplace share a certain social identity, there is a growing opportunity to organize them. Maureen Scully and Amy Segal studied how employee activist groups in one high-tech firm negotiated changes in working conditions, career pathways, and broader issues of power within the corporation. These groups represented female, African-American, Asian-American, gay, lesbian, bisexual, and aging employees.

Their primary accomplishments included increasing the aware-ness of diversity, mobilizing events to make the work environment more comfortable for traditionally marginalized and less power-ful employees, improving retention and promotion opportunities, and changing the style of work and the allocation of power. For example, the African-American Caucus pressed the company to appoint black managers in its emerging South African operation and lobbied to have a person of color appointed to the company's board of directors, and the Gay and Lesbian Alliance researched the costs and the structure of same-sex-partner benefits and worked with human-resources professionals to get these benefits provided. The latter group also lobbied (successfully) to move the company's annual sales conference from Colorado to California after Colorado passed an amendment denying civil-rights protec-tion on the basis of sexual orientation.

Social-identity groups have grown in number and in variety. One estimate suggests that about one-third of the Fortune 500 firms have such groups.[22] Even IBM, a company that is well known for avoiding any form of group or collective process that might serve as an incubator for union activity, now reports hav-ing more than 70 identity groups in place, 30 of which are women's groups.[23] Some firms have worked effectively with social-identity groups and now encourage their efforts. Others, however, fear the loss of control these groups might encourage. At a recent meeting of human-resources executives from large firms, opinions of social-identity groups were evenly split between executives who argued that they and their managerial colleagues saw such groups as consistent with a culture of pro-moting participation and change from the bottom up and those who reported that they and their managerial colleagues saw such groups as threatening. Our further discussions with leaders of social-identity groups and with corporate executives suggest that the groups that are most successful in promoting and achieving change and in advancing the careers of their members work within the prevailing organizational culture and help members navigate within that culture while working slowly and perhaps unconsciously to change it.

Conclusion

As the examples presented in this chapter suggest, a great deal of experimentation with new approaches is occurring in unions and professional organizations and in other groups not directly affiliated with the labor movement that serve some of the functions of unions. To date, however, these efforts have not done much to reverse organized labor's decline. For example, even though 73,000 new members were recruited into the building-trades unions in 1997, the percentage of employees organized in this sector increased by only 0.1. In 1998, construction unions lost 11,000 workers, amounting to 1 percent of their membership. Although the CWA gained new members by diversifying into white-collar occupations other outside its original charter, its membership continues to be concentrated in the traditional (and shrinking) wire-line segment of the industry, particularly among traditional craft workers and service and sales workers in local exchange carriers. The SEIU, though it has made strides in organizing physicians and home-care workers, also has been unable to reverse its decline. In the 1990s, the SEIU spent considerable sums of money on organizing (combined spending by locals and the international union increased from less than $20 million in 1995 to more than $60 million in 1998) and recruited record numbers of new members (38,000 in 1996, 81,000 in 1997, 185,000 in 1998); however, since a significant number of these "new" members resulted from mergers with other unions (144,000 in 1997 and 1998 alone), even these successes are indications of the difficulties that unions face.

Each of the innovative efforts described here can contribute to the building of next-generation unions, but they are independent, isolated efforts. As far as we know, no effort is being made to think about how they might be linked to create a network of opportunities for representing workers throughout their working lives. This is a natural opportunity for the labor movement. But if the labor movement doesn't take it on, other organizations will likely step in and fill the void in a manner that may or may not be sympathetic to labor's broader objectives and role in society.

To pursue the opportunity, unions will have to do a number of things simultaneously.

First, they will have to continue to serve their traditional constituency. That is, they will have to continue to organize workers who are mistreated on their jobs, who distrust their employers, and who see collective bargaining as a way to achieve justice and improved employment standards. This is the bedrock responsibility of any labor movement, and the American labor movement has clearly signaled its continued commitment to it.

Second, to meet the preferences and the needs of a more representative cross-section of the work force, unions must move to an organizing and recruiting strategy and image that reaches individuals outside their core constituency—those who are not necessarily distrustful of their employer but who want and would benefit from an independent institution that would strengthen their voice, help them achieve dignity, increase their opportunity to learn and develop new skills, and enhance their sense of professionalism. In order for unions to achieve these outcomes, there will have to be changes in labor law. There will also have to be changes in how unions view employee participation. Instead of seeing employee participation as a way for employers to compete for workers' loyalties and to avoid unionization, unions will have to appropriate it and become visible champions and skilled facilitators of employee voice at work.

Such an approach will open up a large new "market" for union membership and services.

Third, unions will have to address the needs of workers in jobs of uncertain duration and those of workers who expect to move from firm to firm multiple times in their careers. This will require them to adopt the occupational, craft, and professional models of organizing and to view union membership as a lifelong commitment and relationship in which the union provides services aimed at maintaining members' employability and their access to changing job opportunities. This is why we suggest that unions might want to adopt the university model, whereby once admitted as a student an individual becomes a member of a university's extended community for life. Many a worker is a member of a union at some point in his or her work life; however, each time a worker leaves a union job, it is likely that he or she will have to be organized again in future jobs. Indeed, national surveys report that there are nearly twice as many former union members in the labor force as there are current union members. Imagine the numbers and the power that unions would gain if they could retain these individuals for life by providing services tailored to their changing needs.

Consider the following hypothetical vignettes of workers in the four segments of the labor market discussed earlier in this chapter.

Mobile Professional

A high school student gets a part-time job in a store and becomes a member of the United Food and Commercial Workers or some other union with collective bargaining representation rights or, in the absence of a contract, she becomes an associate member of a union. Upon high school graduation, she becomes eligible for a union-funded college scholarship and/or a low-interest loan, and she is assigned a mentor who is available to advise her on personal, educational, and career matters. The mentor is supported by a career resource center staffed and supported through the local labor movement's central labor council. The center has state-of-the-art vocational- and career-guidance software and staff specialists, and it puts on career fairs and other informational and educational events that are open to high school students and recent graduates. While in college, the student continues to receive union publications, and she has access to an information service that matches students with summer jobs. As she approaches graduation, information on her major is referred to the union and/or to the professional associations most closely linked to her chosen field. They welcome her as a member of their student network and provide information on career opportunities and on the representational services they organizations provide. Upon taking her first job after college, she will be offered an associate membership in the appropriate union or association and given the opportunity to network with others in her area who are employed in the same field. If the organization she works for is unionized, she is encouraged (if not required by a union security clause) to join that union. If no union with collective bargaining rights is present, she will be given support and resources, and encouraged to work with her peers, to organize the work site or organization for this purpose. In any event, she will remain an associate union member, she will continue to receive information on union activities and information on the job market, and she will be encouraged to request technical assistance from her union if and when issues come up on the job that could best be addressed by group efforts (e.g., proposing new family and work benefits or policies, promoting employee participation, comparing leave or educational benefit provisions). She will also have the opportunity to contribute to an individual benefits fund (similar to a 401(k)), managed by a union consortium, that she may use at some later date to take time off from work for further education and/or for maternity leave or child care. Continuing education opportunities would also be provided by the union, along with various group health insurance, 401(k) or related pension plan programs, and other financial discounts. If she takes a maternity leave or takes time off to care for her children, she can draw on benefits that have accrued in her account. If she moves across jobs, occupations, or geographic areas, similar "handoffs" will allow her to transfer her membership from one union, professional association, or local labor council to another. All this time, she will be counted as a member of the labor movement, encouraged to pursue collective bargaining rights for herself and her peers and to support the efforts of others doing so, and encouraged to volunteer in support of local or national causes.

Worker in a Low-Income Job

For a young worker who decides to enter the labor market directly out of high school, or for a new immigrant entering the labor market through a low-income job, the network model will have to extend beyond the boundaries of traditional unions to include a variety of community, religious, ethnic, cultural, educational, and training organizations and institutions. (BUILD in Baltimore and similar coalitions in other cities are useful models.) These organizations and institutions will have to be linked to active organizing efforts, as was the case with the home-care workers in Los Angeles. To provide opportunities for upward occupational mobility, these efforts will have to be combined with continuing education and training programs. Furthermore, serving the full range of needs of low-income families requires negotiating through collective bargaining and through state and local government political channels for expanded family and child care and development benefits and services.

Contingent Worker

Strategies for representing contingent workers can be built on the models being tested by Working Today, by the South Bay Labor Council, and by several other central labor councils. Their long-term contributions to rebuilding the labor movement lie not only in the representation they provide to employees in contingent jobs but also in the extent to which they build a sustaining relationship with these workers and organizational links to other parts of the labor movement so that the worker remains a part of the labor movement when he or she moves to a more permanent job.

Worker in the Core Constituency

Finally, consider a worker employed in an industry that is partially unionized, as are most industries in the United States today. Early in his career, this worker is likely to work for a variety of employers before settling into a longer-term relationship. Even after settling in, he will be constantly at risk that his skills will atrophy as technologies change, that his organizational unit will be restructured or reorganized in ways that change his job and his work, that his work will be outsourced to another firm, or that the demand for the products or services his unit provides will be lost to some domestic or global competitor. Some of the employers for whom this individual will work will have collective bargaining relationships; some will not. And the employers will vary in managerial ideology and in degree of resistance to unions.

Collective bargaining will continue to be the central strategy for representing core-constituency workers. Getting collective bargaining coverage for a significantly larger percentage of workers in these more standard employment relationships will require efforts to gain neutrality from employers and/or changes in labor law that limit illegal tactics and lower the level of conflict associated with gaining collective bargaining rights. But our prototypical industrial employee also will want to have a direct voice at the workplace. His union, therefore, will have to be a champion for employee voice and participation and will have to have its own model for the forms of workplace redesign and labor-management partnership that best fit the features of its industry and its technological environment. He will also need to have access to ongoing educational opportunities to keep his skills current in case he has to reenter the external labor market. His union will therefore have to provide lifelong educational and training programs linked to community colleges and universities and available to all associate members. Job-market information databases and networks tied to these programs will allow workers to compare their wages, working conditions, and promotion opportunities against industry standards and benchmarks. Moreover, the data aggregated in these industry data banks could be used to publicize the differences in employment standards and conditions offered by different firms in the community, in the industry, and in the global supply chain. These services would be aimed at building the loyalty of members so that they retain their membership if they move from one job to another.

Summary

Next-generation unions will have to employ different but complementary strategies to recruit, organize, represent, and retain members. They will not be able to do this alone. They will have to form and maintain coalitions with community groups and other workers' advocacy groups. They will have to work to reduce the costs of organizing to employers; in return (or, in some cases, through the use of union power), employers' opposition to organizing will have to be neutralized. From the federal government, unions will need economic changes, regulatory changes, and changes in labor policy that will give unions and their future members access to the jobs of the new economy.

These various functions will not necessarily be performed by single organizations. There may be specialization—core competencies, if you will. Some unions may choose to organize in traditional ways, relying on things that have traditionally motivated employees, while new organizations, professional associations, and networks recruit, represent, and service members in new ways. We believe this would be a second-best solution. But if this turns out to be the case, there will have to be active strategies for cooperation and mutual respect among unions, professional organizations, and others organizations yet to be invented. The labor movement might be seen as coordinating the work of different groups, and that is why we see next-generation unions as extended networks of groups and organizations through which individuals flow.

If this vision of the next-generation unions is to become a reality. at least three things will have to change. First, unions will have to expand the ways they recruit and retain members. They will have to recruit individuals and stay with them over their careers rather than limit their organizing to the all-or-nothing 50 percent majority it now takes to get one new member. Second, substantial change in labor law will be needed to make it possible for unions to play these different roles effectively. Third, American management culture will have change significantly to accept the simple idea that workers should have the same freedom of association at work as they have in civil society. The last may be the biggest hurdle.

5

The Emergence of New Institutions

Just as the New Deal made assumptions about the nature of employees and the characteristics of jobs and careers, it made some assumptions about the key "players," assigning central roles to government, business, and unions. It was assumed that policies in regard to labor law, job training, and the regulation of standards would be built around these three institutions. The assumptions were natural and sensible in view of the size and the importance of these three institutions; indeed, at the time of the New Deal they represented a clear step toward acknowledging the legitimacy of multiple constituencies in shaping economic outcomes.

We agree that government, business, and unions are major actors, and we have devoted a substantial part of our discussion to their evolving role. However, it is also important to recognize that in recent years new organizations have emerged in local, regional, and international labor markets. Community groups, education and training coalitions, and temporary-help firms and other job-matching entities are playing significant roles and have the potential to become even more important over time. Indeed, we believe that the reconstruction of America's labor-market institutions must take these organizations into account and must build on their potential.

We will group the activities of these new labor-market organizations into three interrelated categories.

The first is advocacy. These organizations represent both individuals and communities in regard to wages and access to jobs.
Some groups organize directly around the role of employee; others are organized by gender or by other status (e.g., immigrants
or gays). To some extent, these groups fulfill functions that are
traditionally the province of unions; however, in some respects
their ambit is broader than that of a union (that is, their basis
for organizing is broader) and in some respects it is narrower
(for example, such groups rarely get involved in how firms organize work).

The second function of these groups is training and lifelong
learning. Recent years have witnessed the emergence of numerous locally based organizations concerned with skill. Some of
these are employer based; others are linked to the advocacy
groups mentioned above.

Third, the increased turnover and mobility in the labor market—a trend that we have repeatedly emphasized—creates a need
for institutions that can effectively match individuals with jobs.
A wide variety of such institutions, including the temporary-help
industry, Web sites, and community organizations, have emerged
to try to meet this need.

Worker Advocacy Groups and Organizations

Throughout the United States, a range of organizations, many
at the community level, are increasingly important (and in some
cases effective) advocates for various concerns of workers. Some
of these organizations work with unions. In fact, the line
between unions and some of these organizations is becoming
rather blurry. Some of the organizations discussed in the previous chapter, such as Working Today, could just as easily have

been introduced here. The difference between traditional unions and most of the organizations discussed in this chapter is that the latter stop at the doors of specific employers. That is, they seek to influence the policies of employers and/or government from outside the workplace, through political channels or other means. Operating below the level of national labor-market policy, these organizations have become important players in some geographic areas.

Immigrant Groups

Immigrant-rights groups are one broad category of such organizations. A compelling example is the Workplace Project, organized on Long Island in 1992.[1] That project worked with immigrants (many undocumented) from South and Central America who were working in low-level service jobs. Because of their vulnerability, employers were paying them below the statutory minimum wage and were also violating federal and state employment regulations in various other ways. Through community organizing and education, the Workplace Project succeeded in organizing these immigrants to launch a campaign aimed at obtaining New York State legislation to strengthen enforcement and increase penalties against employers who violated the law. The low status of the immigrants and the structure of the New York legislature (which is dominated by conservative rural upstate representatives) made this project seem quixotic, yet it succeeded in both passing legislation and improving the state's enforcement system.

The Industrial Areas Foundation Model

The Workplace Project operated in one community. An example of a group of community organizations operating on a large scale and seeking to transform the labor market in their respective areas is the Industrial Areas Foundation, a national network of 40 organizations representing more than a thousand institutions and a million families throughout the United States. In each locality the organization is independent and governed by local leadership, but the network shares a common philosophy of organizing and comes together frequently to share strategies and experiences. Many of the organizations have emphasized labor-market strategies; indeed, the nation's first living-wage campaign was organized by BUILD.

In a number of areas, including San Antonio, Austin, El Paso, Dallas, and the Rio Grande Valley, the Industrial Areas Foundation has been active in establishing labor-market intermediaries. Like conventional employment and training programs, they provide skills and they actively design their training to meet the needs of local employers. Unlike conventional programs, they also seek to change the structure of the labor market and to bargain with employers on behalf on their constituencies. We will illustrate this point with a description of one such intermediary: a job training initiative called Project QUEST in San Antonio.

Most accounts date the momentum for the development of Project QUEST from the January 1990 announcement of the closing of a Levi Strauss & Company plant that had employed more than 1000. After this closure, two local IAF organizations, Communities Organized for Public Service (COPS) and Metro Alliance, began to investigate the economic situation of their members. At first, COPS and Metro Alliance sought to develop a grass-roots understanding of the ongoing economic dislocation. That effort began with house meetings in which one or more IAF leaders would visit the members of affiliated organizations in their homes. Other community members were typically also invited. Between four and fifteen people attended each house meeting.

An important aspect of the efforts of the IAF's leaders was generating support for their emergent job training initiative from the San Antonio business community. They began by getting a few influential employers committed to the initiative; then they leveraged those commitments in larger meetings of business leaders. Ultimately a large number of employers expressed commitment to the training, promising to provide information on their evolving staffing requirements, to cooperate in curriculum development, and to offer financial or other support.

At the core of the QUEST model are several distinctive features. The program began with a commitment from firms to provide jobs for the graduates. (The IAF's power in San Antonio was obviously crucial to obtaining this.) The training was long term. Although full stipends were not provided, various forms of financial support were available, as were intensive counseling and various kinds of support. The training itself took place at community colleges, and QUEST worked with those colleges (again drawing on the power of the IAF organizations) to redesign their curricula and their remediation efforts in various ways. QUEST insisted that all job placements meet a living-wage standard. In addition, QUEST worked with employers to develop job ladders.

A 1996 evaluation demonstrated that QUEST led to substantial gains for its participants. The estimated annual increase in earnings was between $4900 and $7500, and the costs were expected to be paid off in only 3 years.[2] As of January 2001, a total of 1370 individuals had graduated from QUEST. About 60 percent of QUEST placements were in health care, and that percentage has remained stable.

Living-Wage Coalitions
The first living-wage campaign was a 1994 campaign in Baltimore that was jointly organized by the American Federation of State, County, and Municipal Employees and the local IAF affiliate, Baltimoreans United in Leadership Development. Since

then, campaigns in about 50 US cities have been organized by various unions and community groups.

The typical living-wage campaign identifies a target group (usually city employees or employees of contractors working for the city) and sets a living wage for them which is above the state or federal minimum wage. An example of this is the living-wage campaign in the Rio Grande Valley of Texas, which began when Valley Interfaith (an Industrial Areas Foundation organization) got involved in the passage of a half-cent sales tax in the city of McAllen. In return for their support of this measure (which had repeatedly failed and which finally passed with Valley Interfaith's support), the organization insisted on a voice in how the funds were to be spent. Out of a series of house meetings there emerged an agenda that included support for a training program modeled on Project QUEST, a branch library, recreation centers, and after-school programs. New tax revenue was also earmarked for school construction. With this success in hand, Valley Interfaith began to think about how the construction funds would be spent. It focused on the question of a living wage. The leaders began a study and came to the conclusion that a living wage was indeed an important issue. In March 1998, at a meeting attended by 7000 people, elected officials agreed in principle to support a living-wage policy. The initial strategy was to target construction jobs associated with the building of schools. Indeed, Valley Interfaith did considerable research into the economics of the local construction industry and its wage-setting practices. In the face of opposition, they asked the attorney general of Texas for an opinion as to the legality of their efforts. The attorney general ruled that living-wage ordinances were acceptable under the Texas constitution but that state legislative action was required to make them permissible. The IAF set about organizing efforts to pass such legislation. In the interim, Valley Interfaith decided, it would target the employees of school districts.

In August 1998, Valley Interfaith succeeded in McAllen and the school district raised the wages of 400 full-time workers from the minimum wage to $7.50 an hour. Similar campaigns meet with success in Pharr, San Juan, and Alamo. These were all administrative decisions by school committees. In June 1999, Valley Interfaith got an ordinance passed in Hidalgo County raising the wages of 1000 county employees, and shortly thereafter the Brownsville School District raised its wages. As direct results of these campaigns, 8500 individuals have had their wages increased. The success of these efforts is impressive and even startling in view of the long history of low-wage employment and the relative powerlessness of poor people in the region.

Living-wage campaigns have two logics, one economic and one political. The economic logic is that the campaigns seek to establish a new base-line "going" wage for adults in the community which is above the federal or state minimum wage. It may be acknowledged that the minimum wage is acceptable for young people and for others whose attachment to the labor market is casual; however for adults whose earnings are important for family support the minimum wage is unacceptable. The power to establish a base-line "going" wage lies partly in legislation (for example, in requirements that city contractors pay the living wage) and partly in shifts of expectations. A long line of research on wage setting shows that expectations can play an important role in local labor markets.

The political logic of living-wage campaigns has to do with their role as an organizing tool. First, the beginning of a campaign provides a stimulus for people to research their local economy and learn about the wage structure. Establishing an initial ordinance then provides a goal around which considerable energy can be mobilized. Once a living wage has gained a foothold through the ordinance, it is possible to approach a new group of workers and ask them whether they realize they are not being paid the living wage. This provides a basis for organization.

Advocates of Work/Family Policies and Practices

Perhaps the largest coalition of groups advocating for workers consists of groups that promote expansion of family benefits and family-friendly workplace policies and practices. The leading political force behind passage of the 1993 federal Family and Medical Leave Act was the Women's Legal Defense Fund, a national organization devoted to promoting and defending women's legal rights in a variety of economic and social settings, including the workplace. Its leaders actively worked toward the passage of this bill for 9 years. Having changed its name to the National Partnership for Women and Families, that organization is now the leading advocate for state legislation to use unemployment-insurance or disability-insurance funds to support paid family leave. But it is not the only organization of this sort. Twenty-one women's organizations (including groups representing low-wage immigrant workers, the Coalition of Labor Union Women, and groups representing professionals and entrepreneurs) came together in 1994 to testify in support of changes in labor law before a federal commission.

The work/family issue has spawned a number of highly visible and active non-profit research and consulting organizations (including Work Family Directions, Catalyst, and the Families and Work Institute) that work with companies to promote adoption and expansion of family-friendly benefits and practices.[3] Clearly they are a force for innovation in the corporate world. Thus, there are multiple "new" voices promoting change by varied means, including lobbying for new legislation, research and education, network building among professionals, and consulting with employers.

Education, Training, and Lifelong-Learning Organizations

Workers' advocacy groups are not alone in seeking to develop new labor-market institutions. In view of the growing importance of knowledge, skill, and continuous training or learning, it is not surprising that the range of groups and organizations that address these matters appears to be expanding. Most of these are more focused on building or keeping current the skills of individual workers or groups than on altering power relationships or changing employers' behavior. In fact, employer groups are either leaders or partners in most of these efforts, since, to be effective, training must be tightly linked to immediate or foreseeable skill requirements. Employers set these requirements and therefore know them best.

Among the earliest and the best-known initiatives along these lines are the programs developed by the Boston Private Industry Council to improve the youth labor market and the transition from school to work. Private Industry Councils (and the related new Regional Employment Boards created by the recently enacted Workforce Investment Act) are community-based bodies made up of employers, local government officials, educators, and labor representatives. The Boston effort began in 1982 with the Boston Compact, a commitment by employers to provide a job to every graduate of Boston's high schools. The underlying idea was to provide an incentive for young people to stay in school. Although it does not seem to have had much of an effect on the high school dropout rate, the program was successful over many years and over different stages in the business cycle in providing the jobs to which it was committed. Over time, the commitment by the Boston business community—operating through the Private Industry Council (PIC)—to creating new youth labor-market institutions has evolved and grown. One of the most notable efforts is the creation of a strong apprenticeship-style program, Project ProTech, in fields such as health and financial services. High school students work in cooperating firms both during the school year and during the summer, and their school curriculum is at least in part organized around material from the jobs. The PIC also provides considerable staff support to the employers and to the students. After graduation the students are able, should they wish, to continue in a community college program in the same field. Other students may leave the occupational cluster and move on to four-year colleges. The business community has also organized college scholarship funds. Beyond Project ProTech, the PIC has developed a sophisticated methodology to mediate between students and employers. In each of Boston's high schools the PIC has placed job developer/counselors who help students navigate the job market and who work with employers to find placements and to help them deal with the young people. This model appears to be quite successful and is being extended, with some modification, to out-of-school youth.

In other communities, business coalitions have sought to reform and reconstruct the entire network of job training programs. A good example is the Cleveland Jobs and Workforce Initiative. That effort was led by the Cleveland Growth Association, an organization of the top 50 firms in the city. The underlying view was that firms were being poorly served by the current employment and training system and that the difficulties lay in programmatic and geographic fragmentation. The Cleveland Growth Association recruited 100 business executives and conducted a year-long series of seminars and trips to examine the best practices elsewhere in the United States; it also convened working groups on topics such as labor exchange and links between training and economic development. This was an entirely business-based effort. There was no attempt in the initial stages to build a broad-based coalition.

The Cleveland Jobs and Workforce Initiative had three broad programmatic goals: to address labor shortages, to develop more customer responsive systems, and to upgrade basic skills. With respect to the first objective, the Initiative established a series of customized and sectoral training programs for groups of firms.[4] These programs are all aimed at individuals who pass entry tests; little in the way of case management is provided for people in difficulty. In addition, a training center has been established for currently employed workers, whom firms can enroll for a small fee. In addition to these programs, the Cleveland Jobs and Workforce Initiative has encouraged the establishment of one-stop career centers and has set up "response teams" within these centers to help firms fill large job orders.

The federal, state, and local governments play important roles in fostering and coordinating institutions such as those described above. The 1998 Workforce Investment Act, for example, specifically requires that 51 percent of the seats on the Regional Employment Boards are allocated to local employers, thus not only ensuring their active partnership but also, in effect, giving employers control over these training institutions. Since 1998, the US Department of Labor has issued grants to a number of local partnerships of business, labor, and community officials aimed at promoting common standards and skill training for workers in particular sectors or industries. Labor leaders are taking the initiative in promoting these local networks and applying for federal funds to support them. The national-level AFL-CIO Center for Workplace Democracy works with local union leaders to build cross-employer, industry-specific partnerships to support such efforts.

The best-known and arguably the most successful of these efforts is the Wisconsin Regional Training Partnership, a consortium of manufacturers, unions, and public-sector partners in the Milwaukee metropolitan area. The Partnership includes 40 employers in metalworking, electronics, plastics, and related industries which together employ roughly 40,000 workers. "At the core of the Partnership," Annette Bernhardt and Thomas Bailey note, "are a series of channels for active communication and planning between employers and unions, for example working groups focused on plant modernization, and peer advisor networks to share best practices. Most of the employers either have or will have an on-site training center that provides continuous training and skill upgrading. A key component is the development of industry-specific skill standards, by employers, unions, and technical colleges in the region. Such standards have been successfully implemented at the entry level, and certificates to improve skill portability across firms are planned. In addition, the Partnership has embarked on two major initiatives to systematize access to entry-level jobs (a youth apprenticeship program and a training program for inner city residents)."[5]

In many parts of the United States, new networks of firms, community colleges, and sometimes unions have emerged. These networks combine an interest in promoting the competitiveness of companies with an interest in facilitating movement through the labor market and improving employment outcomes for people at risk. The three basic building blocks are training programs, labor-market intermediaries, and manufacturing extension services. The latter are modeled on the old idea of the agriculture extension service; some are funded by the federal government under the auspices of the National Institutes of Standards and Technology (NIST) and some are funded by state governments. Experts (often industrial engineers or retired executives) help firms (usually small and medium-size ones) to solve technical problems involving such matters as plant layout, inventory systems, implementation of quality programs, and installation of new technology. In the course of this, the best of the extension services also help the employers upgrade their human-resources systems.

A fully developed effort would bring employers together to discuss common technical, marketing, and employment problems and to find resources with which to solve them, would engage these employers in designing common training programs, and would create a mechanism to enable individuals to move easily from one firm to another. In this way, a network of institutions would be created that would provide structure for the local labor market.

Some of the networks are business driven, a good example being the efforts of the National Tooling and Machining Association. In Western Massachusetts and in seven other areas around the United States, the NTMA has organized small machine shops into a network that trains young entrants, provides further training for incumbent employees, shares technical information, and acts as an informal clearing house for job seekers. The Western Massachusetts Precision Institute trains about 100 new machinists and about 200 incumbent employees a year in addition to performing the other "networking" tasks listed above. Similar networks have been created under union auspices. An example is the Garment Industry Development Corporation in New York, which is affiliated with the Union of Needletrades, Industrial and Technical Employees. The GIDC is a well-established operation that runs on-site training for operators throughout New York's large garment industry, provides training for employees dislocated from the industry, runs a marketing and technical assistance service for managers, and has established a job referral system called JOBNET. Networks can also be created directly by public authorities. In 1994, according to one estimate, 27 states were supporting 140 networks.[6] In addition, roughly 100 manufacturing extension service centers have been created through the federal NIST program (housed in the Department of Commerce). These efforts are heterogeneous, and a good many are purely engineering driven with few labor-market components. Others are broad ranging and share many of the characteristics of the GDIC.

The importance of lifelong learning is attracting the attention of a host of organizations that traditionally were not considered labor-market intermediaries. Universities all around the United States (and in other parts of the world) are exploring the question of what role they should play in distance education, in continuing education, or in lifelong learning. Some are doing this on their own and are focusing mainly on their alumni or on adult workers in their local communities; others are expanding the number of partnership arrangements they have with industry to support teaching, research, technology development and innovation, and continuing education. The Massachusetts Institute of Technology, for example, has historically had many links to industry through research centers, laboratories, and consortia, and it has expanded the range of its links through programs such as Leaders for Manufacturing (LFM) and System Design and Management (SDM). These are jointly governed university-industry partnerships that grant advanced MS degrees to engineers. Similar programs exist and/or are expanding in many other universities today. The future is likely to see a growing role for colleges and universities in lifelong learning and distance education.

Job-Matching Organizations

Most of the institutions engaged in job matching operate as for-profit companies. This is particularly true of the temporary-help industry, the most rapidly expanding industry in the labor market over the past two decades. Between 1970 and 1995 this industry grew at an annual rate of 11 percent—5 times as fast as non-farm employment.[7]

Temporary-help firms differ in character from the activities of community groups and business groups in the labor market. The community groups have no profit motive whatsoever; the motives of the business groups described above, while linked to improving firm performance, do so through indirect means and are not concerned with the well-being of any specific enterprise. Nonetheless, temporary-help firms are important to discuss in the current context, because the industry has emerged as an innovative labor-market intermediary.

Temporary-help firms have been increasingly important to the operation of firms, in some cases having taken over a number of the human-resources management functions. In recent years the industry has matured and become more central to a wider range of employer activities. Increasingly temporary-help firms take responsibility for an entire work function (for example, call centers that handle customer relations). Illustrative of this trend is a recent agreement between Manpower Inc. and Ameritech. Those two firms plan to jointly seek call-center business, Manpower supplying the people and Ameritech providing the technology. Outsourcing of call centers is increasing at a rate of between 20 percent and 40 percent a year.[8] According to one source, the percentage of the revenues of temporary-help agencies attributable to vendor-on-premises agreements grew from 2 percent in 1992 to 11 percent in 1996.[9]

Temporary-help firms also act as labor-market intermediaries, playing a new and major role in the hiring process. In effect, they recruit and screen employees for the enterprise, and in doing so they relieve the firm of the risks that can be associated with a formal probationary period. For example, a number of temporary-help firms have formed alliances with outplacement firms to help find jobs for displaced middle managers.

More generally, temporary-help firms have become an important element in the recruiting process. In the 1997 Survey of Establishments, the bulk of temporary employees were reportedly associated with an establishment for short durations: 62.9 percent of establishments said the typical length of employment was less than 6 months, while 24.6 percent said it was between

6 and 12 months. However, a non-trivial fraction eventually get hired by the establishment (23.8 percent for agency temporaries). It is therefore clear that these agencies have emerged as an important, and new, labor-market institution.

More recently, tight labor markets for employees with strong skills in software development or Web-site design, and for those with related information-processing skills, have encouraged the emergence of Internet-based placement companies, such as Monster.com. One organization, Eworks Exchange, specializes in matching independent contractors and consultants possessing information-technology skills with employers having specific project requirements. In addition to serving as a match-making institution, Eworks gives contractors an opportunity to buy group health insurance and a 401(k) savings plan. In the course of their normal business activity, Eworks, Manpower, and similar firms gather an enormous amount of data on skill requirements, on the supply of specialized skills, and on the gaps between supply and demand. Some of these organizations use this information to design education and training programs to close the supply-demand gap.

Summary and Conclusions

We began this chapter by arguing that new institutional forms in local and regional labor markets hold considerable promise as building blocks of a new labor market. Now that we have reviewed some representative initiatives, it is useful to step back and assess their implications for labor-market policy.

Each of the initiatives described above is aimed at changing how labor markets work. For this reason, and because of their impressive successes and the tremendous energy behind them, we consider them to be elements of a reconstructed labor market. At the same time, some important qualifications are necessary.

First, the initiatives are not all alike. For example, temporary-help firms, although they are important players, operate purely from a profit motive and have little interest in issues of equity. From the viewpoint of policy, probably the most interesting thing to be learned from those firms is that there is a strong demand for their services (which implies that firms need intermediaries).

The second qualification is that the new institutions are limited in scope. Even with their considerable power, the Industrial Areas Foundation organizations are not involved in discussions of careers, health and safety, work/family issues, or even internal training. They do not, at least thus far, address the kinds of concerns that are typically the province of workplace-based unions. In addition, most of these institutions are local and regional. Although the local and regional stages are important, many crucial decisions are made, and debates played out, at the national level. Hence, we should rethink labor-market institutions nationally, not merely locally.

Finally, not all of these new labor-market institutions will survive. One reason is the funding base of many of these organizations. The IAF has a relatively stable base of churches, but many of the new community-based groups rely on uncertain and unreliable funding. Nor do we know much yet about their effectiveness. We may be at such an early stage in the development of many of these institutions that the best government policy would be to support them to the point where they can be evaluated carefully for sustainability, performance, and generalizability to other settings. Then, with this information in hand, those that pass these tests could be targeted for diffusion to a scale large enough to benefit the overall national economy.

6

Recasting the Role of Government

The New Deal established the federal government as the main regulator of the labor market and of employment relations in the United States. This was due both to the emergence of national markets and to the view that old assumptions, which we laid out in chapter 1, would come to characterize the entire labor market in a relatively uniform way. Today a different starting assumption for the role of government is needed. Globalization has undermined the preeminence of the federal government as a regulator of employment practices and outcomes, since many of the powers it once exercised are now lodged in international agencies. Paradoxically, the importance of regional, state, and local governments has increased. Finally, the labor market is far more diverse than it was when the New Deal system was constructed. Taken together, these shifts require a new vision of the role of the federal government.

The vision we lay out in this chapter builds on the innovations occurring among the other labor-market actors discussed throughout the volume. We envision the federal government supporting and complementing these innovations and helping them achieve a scale large enough to benefit the overall economy and society. Moreover, we suggest that the federal government's regulatory roles and enforcement strategies be modernized to accommodate and take advantage of the diversity of today's economy and today's employment relationships. We see what we are proposing as a new way of linking government, employers, unions, community groups, and labor-market intermediaries efforts to address the labor-market challenges of our time.

The New Architecture

Government is in many ways the most complex of the major socio-economic actors. It plays multiple roles. It is a direct provider of important labor-market and social services, including education, training, social insurance, public assistance, and family support. At the same time, it creates the institutional and regulatory framework in which the other actors interact. It provides a forum for public debate and discussion. At its best, it provides leadership and strategic direction for the evolution of the system.

In each of these roles, moreover, government is not a unitary actor. Its power is dispersed among local, state, and federal governments and, increasingly, shared with international agencies and regulatory bodies. At each of these levels, power is further divided among the legislative, executive, and judicial branches. And at the federal level executive power is dispersed among numerous cabinet departments and administrative agencies, each with considerable autonomy.

Despite this complexity, in the postwar system that grew out of the New Deal social legislation the federal government was the preeminent governmental actor. Its role was active and direct, and the national economy prospered as a unit. Localities and states were dependent on national markets, and it was the responsibility of the federal government to create and maintain such markets and ensure their stability. One of the major products of the shifts in the social and economic environment that we have been examining in this volume is a fundamental change in the relative power and responsibility of the various governmental jurisdictions—a change that led to a shift in the relative importance of the various roles that governmental actors play.

In the new economy, prosperity is more and more dependent on the international economy, and the power and responsibility to ensure it is lodged in multinational agencies such as the European Commission, the International Monetary Fund, the World Bank, the International Labor Organization, and the World Trade Organization. Paradoxically, globalization has also increased the importance of localities and subnational regions; states and localities are increasingly able to prosper on their own, finding niches in the international market or even economies of scale in multinational markets, independently of the health of the nations where they are located. State and local governments have responsibility for the development and implementations of the strategies that enable them to do so.

But the federal government remains a major player. It is central to the ability of both international agencies and subnational governments to play their roles effectively with regard to the United States. Its role now is less one of direct action than one of providing financial support, strategic direction, and leadership for other governmental actors. Since we are living in a period of transition, and since the hallmark of the emergent economic order is diversity, the federal role in this regard lies less in championing particular institutions and practices than in mobilizing resources, encouraging experimentation, facilitating comparison and evaluation of alternative approaches, and diffusing the best practices. We thus begin with a discussion of how the federal government has begun to play this role and how its capacity to do so can be strengthened.

But before we outline how we see government fitting into this new architecture, perhaps we should address a more basic question. In view of the popularity of free-market rhetoric today, some might ask why government should play *any* role in labor-market affairs. Why not just leave it to the market to adjust to changes? The simple answer is that, although both the American public and American policy makers generally favor market solutions in many areas, they have never favored them with respect to labor-market and employment relations issues. Even before the New Deal, and certainly thereafter, society has sought to coordinate labor markets through some combination of market forces, government action, and collective bargaining. This, as we suggested in chapter 1, is because work is a social as well as an economic process, and because work involves important moral values and power relationships that are not always reflected in the unregulated workings of market forces. In short, Americans expect their government to provide a policy environment that reflects their moral values and their sense of fairness, but to do so efficiently, leaving the greatest possible amount of control in the hands of those closest to the problems. This, then, is the task of the new architecture we sketch out here.

Government as a Catalyst for Change

We see government as a catalyst for and a supporter of the changes and innovations discussed throughout this volume. This is consistent with the goal of supporting the decentralized efforts of the actors in the labor market to adapt to and address their problems as they see fit. It also reflects the need to find new ways to work with the international agencies that have the most influence over how globalization proceeds and how it is governed. One important objective of the federal government, therefore, is to sanction and support a greater role for state and local governments and for international agencies and institutions.

With respect to state and local governments and with respect to community or local labor-market groups and organizations, the federal government should foster experimentation, evaluate and disseminate the results, support the development of sustainable funding strategies, and review the emergent institutional structure to ensure the coherence of the system as a whole. This is essentially the process through which the New Deal reforms emerged out of the preceding period. Much more sophisticated techniques of experimentation and evaluation have been developed in the last 20 years in the national debates about social policy, especially in regard to welfare reform and medical insurance, and this places the federal government in a more effective position to play the aforementioned role today. The federal government has in fact been playing this role for some time in the area of employment and training programs and in the area of welfare reform. We believe that its mission should be conceived more broadly to include not only experimentation and the evaluation of program content but also the building of specific institutions and the development of local leadership.

Some of this is already happening. Under the Workforce Investment Act, the Department of Labor has issued requests for proposals to fund local institutions engaged in cross-firm, regional, and sectoral skill development and training programs. The Department of Labor also has announced its willingness to support institutional development—that is, the building of new institutions to perform this linking and training function. As we noted in chapter 5, a number of local union, employer, and government groups are taking advantage of this opportunity. This is exactly the type of approach that should be encouraged, evaluated, and (on the basis of the lessons learned) expanded across the United States.

However, much more is possible. For example, Congress has significantly increased the funding available for training as a part of legislation granting more visas to immigrants who possess scarce information-technology skills. Part of the funding comes from payments required of the employers that sponsor and hire these immigrants. A substantial portion of these funds ($65 million) went unspent in the first year of their availability. Clearly this is an example of a funding mechanism and a body of resources that could be used strategically to support and sustain promising community-level experiments and institutions.

If lifelong learning is (as we and many others have argued) growing in importance, and if individual firms have little economic incentive or ability to ensure that employees keep their general human capital current, government has an important catalytic or coordinating role to play. But it need not do this alone. Since firms collectively have an interest in maintaining a highly skilled work force, the potential exists for building a coordinated private-public pool of resources for lifelong learning. The question is: What are the best ways to finance funds that workers might draw on periodically in the course of their careers to refresh their skills or to learn new skills demanded by technological changes? Perhaps the unemployment insurance system serves as a model for financing such investments. But these funds should accumulate like Social Security funds, regardless of tenure with a specific employer. If the government moves in this direction, it should do so in a way that complements what some firms are already doing to support workers displaced permanently by restructuring or downsizing and the efforts of some firms and unions to create joint training funds and programs that support continuous education and training for employed workers. Joint funds have the attraction of building shared commitment and decentralized, joint administration into the effort. Providing a pool of matching public funds would be one way to encourage more employees and their unions and employers to make these investments.

Other small but significant steps could further encourage broader and more sustained private investments in lifelong learning. A "temporary" provision in the federal tax code allows employers to deduct educational expenditures. A simple change would be to make this a permanent feature of the tax code. A more ambitious effort might explore ways to build individual learning accounts or banked funds akin to individual retirement accounts that would allow workers to take time out to refresh their skills (either by attending classes or by means of distance learning). Encouraging firms, unions, professional associations, colleges, and universities to work together to develop such opportunities for all workers is another way to capitalize on and shape a trend that is already emerging.

A new generation of leaders will have to be developed for the emerging community institutions and for next-generation unions and professional associations. One model for leadership development was created in the 1970s, when the US Occupational Safety and Health Administration recognized a need for more industrial hygienists in industry and in the labor movement. That recognition led to the New Directions Program, which provided grants to unions, industry associations, and other non-profit groups for the development and training of occupational health professionals who could help identify and abate workplace health hazards. The result was a considerable expansion in the capabilities of unions and other organizations to perform these functions.

Another program that can be used to build networks and institutional capacity exists in the labor-management area. Under the 1978 Labor Management Cooperation Act, the Federal Mediation and Conciliation Service is authorized to provide grants to industry-based or local labor-management committees. It has been doing so at a funding level of approximately $1.5 million per year. This program provided seed funding for several of the innovations we discussed in earlier chapters, including the Garment Industry Investment Corporation in New York and the

San Francisco Hotel Industry Association. FMCS mediators have also been active in helping local labor and management groups improve the quality of their relationships. But estimates suggest that FMCS's efforts in this area have reached less than 10 percent of their potential "customers," even though these outreach efforts are rated highly by those served and the majority of labor and management negotiators would like to see these services expanded.[1] This program could be expanded to reach larger numbers and to help the parties create the types of labor-management relationships and practices best suited to the changing work force and economy. It could also be broadened to include the full range of community groups and institutions that have something to contribute to improving the quality of relationships and the pace of innovation in a local area or in a sector of the economy.

These examples are only meant to illustrate some of the options that are available for the federal government to play a constructive and supportive role in sustaining innovations begun locally. What is more important than the specific instruments chosen is the need to see support for these local initiatives as a central part of the federal government's role in the modern labor market.

International Agencies and Institutions

In many ways the process of globalization and the newly emergent economic order is the outstanding success of the US government's leadership and strategic direction. The United States has been the primary force pressing for an open international marketplace. The US government has provided the leadership and the strategic vision for the new international order and has fostered the expansion of trade. And, in the absence of effective international leadership and a central administrative body, the United States has been the major force articulating a direction and coordinating policy among the major international agencies. The institutional and economic structures that govern American capitalism are the template for the international order that is being created. This is especially true of the definition of property rights, both real and intellectual.

However, the US government has conspicuously abrogated its responsibilities for strategic leadership in the area of workers' rights and labor standards. The international accords that the United States has negotiated have either neglected these questions altogether or left workers' rights and labor standards poorly defined and the institutions created to enforce them weak and ineffectual. This is a major limitation of the process of the globalization, and it weakens the legitimacy of the system as a whole.

The particular rights that should be respected in the new global order and the procedures through which these rights should be recognized and enforced are not obvious. Low labor cost is the chief advantage of developing countries competing with the advanced technologies and the extensive capital infrastructure of the United States and other developed countries, and regulations that restrict the organization of labor are an easy pretext for protectionism. Workers' rights have become increasingly precarious in the United States over the last three decades, and the rights of workers abroad have become entrapped in debates about the deterioration of workers' rights at home. Foreign countries are rightly suspicious of a kind of cultural imperialism in which Americans impose their own social standards on places that have elaborate moral codes of their own. On the other hand, it must also be acknowledged that the regulations of the advanced industrial countries reflect their longer experience with modern production technologies and the risks they entail. The complexities here suggest that an effective system of labor standards cannot be unilaterally imposed by the United States. They must grow out of an extensive international debate and experimentation. But the United States can foster that debate and encourage the experimentation. The International Labor Organization, the traditional site for such debates, has the obvious advantage of representing business, labor, and government. But precisely because the representation is institutionalized in this way, it does not always give voice to workers from the informal sectors of the economy, where violations of standards are the biggest problem. It also has a tradition of approaching these problems legalistically with uniform standards that do not typically take account of the variation in moral codes across different cultures and systems of production. In addition, in the newly emergent international order, power is lodged in the International Monetary Fund, the World Trade Organization, and, to a lesser extent, the World Bank. These organizations control the right of access to the international marketplace, and that control could be used to punish violations of standards.

Recently there have been a number of attempts to attack the root causes of unacceptable labor practices (such as the use of child labor) directly rather than through sanctions in trade agreements, side letters, or ILO standards. One such attempt involves paying subsidies to families who send their children to school rather than to work.[2] Another interesting development has been the emergence of consumer boycotts aimed at getting multinational garment and shoe firms to accept responsibility for the employment conditions of their international suppliers and subcontractors. Another example is the growing role of various nongovernmental organizations that propose to monitor and publicize conditions in the factories of garment and shoe contractors.[3] The US government is in a position to encourage and expand these new approaches directly and also less directly through its influence on international funding agencies. And the US government could use its voice in the international arena to disseminate the results and to use them to initiate a debate. At the same time that it encourages debate of these issues, the federal government should be sensitive to concerns about "cultural imperialism."

None of the aforementioned approaches will be successful, however, in the absence of ways to move from monitoring and exposure of practices to enforcement and adjudication of disputes over them that are responsive to indigenous social standards and different stages of economic development. The system of arbitration that grew up in the American system of collective bargaining is one model of how this could be done. This system gained sufficient credibility that the federal courts deferred to arbitrators' judgments in adjudicating disputes over workplace rules. The courts saw these as fair but flexible means for enforcing rules particular to each workplace as determined by arbitrators specially trained to discern indigenous social norms. The European Community has developed another set of mechanisms designed to respect the particular labor codes of its individual members within the framework of a single multinational system. The international community, operating through trans-national organizations, should search for ways such as these to strengthen the capacity of nations to enforce their own standards.

We now turn to a discussion of how government's regulatory role can be adapted to a more mobile, rapidly changing, and diverse economy and labor force. Just as the New Deal model designed policies and institutions to take advantage of and to work with the large integrated firms of the industrial economy, the model we propose here seeks to work with and to take advantage of the institutions that are emerging in the new economy.

Moving Away from Seeing the Firm as the Key Source of Labor-Market Services and Benefits

Throughout this volume we have emphasized the need to shift policies away from reliance on the individual firm as the unit through which labor-market services or functions are performed. The primary reason for this is that a substantial number of workers experience high rates of mobility across firms. An additional reason is that individual firms are less stable today than the integrated industrial enterprises envisioned by the architects of the New Deal employment policies and therefore less able or less willing to perform some of these functions. In this section we outline how such a shift might affect several aspects of labor-market and employment policy.

Modernizing Unemployment Insurance

The policy most important to the quality of labor-market experience in the world of high mobility is unemployment insurance. In general, coverage under the unemployment insurance system has contracted to the point that less than half of the unemployed are covered and less than a third receive benefits. But in addition, the structure of hours requirements in the unemployment insurance system, based as it is on the old image of the labor market, works against the interest of contingent employees. These biases result from the structure of the minimum hours and earnings requirements that most states impose for eligibility. Bassi and McMurrer estimate that, while 93 percent of full-time full-year workers and 93 percent of workers who earn more than $10 per hour meet eligibility requirements, only 42 percent of part-time part year workers and 56 percent of people who earn less than the minimum wage meet them.[4] A report by the Advisory Council on Unemployment Compensation made a number of recommendations aimed at expanding eligibility, basing it on hours worked over a base period (rather than on earnings) and setting the hours threshold at 800 per year. Bassi and McMurrer estimate that these changes might establish eligibility for an additional 15 percent of all unemployed workers.

Unemployment insurance was originally designed to protect workers subject to temporary layoffs due to cyclical or seasonal swings in demand. However, the nature of unemployment has shifted from temporary layoffs to permanent job loss due to restructuring, downsizing, or movement of jobs abroad. The central question for the unemployment insurance system therefore has become whether it should remain a narrowly constructed income-maintenance program or whether it should become a part of a broader effort at structural adjustment. The latter approach would imply the need for unemployment compensation to support investment in training and skills (and perhaps mobility assistance) to help an individual qualify for a new job when his or her job has been eliminated.

A special fund does exist for those who can demonstrate their job has been eliminated because of foreign competition. The Trade Adjustment Act provides extended unemployment benefits and training assistance for workers who are displaced for this particular reason. Although this program may serve as a model, it is often difficult to judge whether international trade is the reason for the job loss. Indeed, there seems little reason to separate out these workers from other workers permanently displaced and in need of adjustment assistance. An expansion of the benefits provided under this program to others in the same situation would seem fair and reasonable.

Promoting Portable Benefits

It is, at least in part, a historical accident that benefits such as health insurance and pensions are employer based in the United States. In the 1920s leading non-union firms seeking to defeat union organizing drives created what came to be known as "welfare capitalism," a system of paternalistic firm-based benefits.[5] Many of these plans died with the onset of the Great Depression,[6] but they did establish at least one image of corporate "best practice." Firm-based benefits received an even stronger impetus during World War II, when a War Labor Board was empaneled by the federal government to suppress wage inflation during a period of severe shortages. However, unions argued successfully that employers could improve benefit packages even when wages were capped. As a result, there were strong incentives to move to an employer-based benefit system. The postwar tax system cemented this arrangement. Employers and employees were allowed to pay their share of benefits in pre-tax dollars. As a result, a dollar of compensation costs that took the form of benefits was worth more than a dollar paid in wages. This tilted the compensation structure toward firm-based benefits.

Today the tax treatment of fringe benefits creates a major problem for those who would adjust the system. To prevent employers from abusing the intent of the tax exemption by providing tax-free compensation in the form of fringe benefits to particular employees, firms are obliged to offer general coverage to all their workers. This requirement creates an incentive for employers to outsource work to temporary workers and to subcontracting companies, for in so doing they can offer fringe benefits to their own employees without covering the "temps" or the employees of subcontractors. A similar incentive is created to employ part-time workers, since fringe benefits are not required for employees working less than 20 hours. These distortions in the incentive structure facing the firm would obviously be reduced if fringe benefits were to be detached from employment.

And firm-based benefits pose two other problems, one that has long been with us and one that is growing in importance.

The long-standing problem is that nothing requires employers to offer benefits, and thus many workers find themselves in jobs that do not provide health insurance or a pension. Put differently, inequality is exacerbated in a firm-based benefits regime because the profile of benefits follows the profile of wages rather than being leveled by government provision. To an extent, this problem has been addressed through the evolution of the Social Security system. Social Security now effectively provides a floor on pensions, and with the addition of Supplementary Social Security coverage is virtually universal. Private pensions supplement Social Security. The newer problem is that firm-based benefits are premised on a fairly low level of inter-firm mobility. When people change jobs with greater frequency or increasingly work in non-standard arrangements, firm-based benefits create difficulties. Losses occur when people move from a firm with coverage to one without. Losses also occur for employees whose pensions are of the defined-benefit variety, because these reward long-term service.

Furthermore, an increasing number of firms do not provide any pensions,[7] and many firms that do have pension plans exclude part-time and contingent workers from participation on the ground that they do not work enough hours per year. Indeed, one can be a full-time worker in the sense of working 2000 hours a year in a series of jobs but not be eligible for a pension at any of the jobs. This is analogous to the problem described above regarding unemployment insurance.

Defined-benefit contribution plans tied to individuals—401(k) plans—would appear to be one solution to these difficulties. These plans are indeed portable. However, a 401(k) plan is useful only if the employee has resources to contribute, and an employer need not contribute unless the employee does. With the older defined-benefit plans, all contributions came from the employer.

A number of ideas are in circulation as to how to deal with the concerns just mentioned. Some are technical fixes, such as reducing the vesting period or permitting employees who leave defined-benefit plans to receive lump sums that they may then invest in 401(k) accounts. Some broader and more powerful ideas also hold promise. For example, in chapter 4 we described Working Today, an organization that enables contingent employees and independent contractors to collectively address problems of health insurance, pensions, and other benefits. Working Today's basic strategy is to build associational health and pension plans much like the TIAA-CREF plans that enable university faculty members to move easily from job to job while retaining their benefits. Moving fully in this direction would require a number of legislative initiatives, such as permitting employees to make pre-tax payments to pension funds even if their employer does not offer a pension plan and permitting the establishment of 401(k) plans not tied to employers.

Medical insurance poses problems similar to those posed by pensions, but there is no floor on coverage comparable to that of the Social Security system. We are reluctant to enter into the complex debate about medical care here, but it should be clear that the labor market has evolved toward detaching coverage from employment altogether and attaching eligibility to the individual, irrespective of his or her employment status.

Though we do not envision a labor force made up entirely of nomadic free agents constantly moving from job to job, increased mobility is a fact of life today and is likely to be so in the future. The common principles of most policies aimed at coping with a mobile labor force are that benefits should be decoupled from tenure with any single employer and that any new government policies promoting broader or uniform coverage should dovetail with what leading firms and their workers are already doing.

Building Institutional Capacity

The New Deal labor policies were premised on the notion that government should establish minimum standards for a limited array of substantive employment outcomes and leave it to collective bargaining and its associated institutions (such as grievance and arbitration) to expand on and move above these minimums. Gradually, however, government regulation of the workplace expanded as unions (and thus the coverage of union grievance procedures) declined. Each of the New Deal statutes has its own regulations and enforcement mechanisms, some of which conflict with others (to the dismay of employers, who are accountable for sorting them out and for ensuring their practices are in compliance). How can we achieve the objectives of the regulations while increasing flexibility and responsiveness?

Clearly, one straightforward solution is to rebuild unions. We support this, and we will suggest policy changes with it in mind. But, in view of the diversity of the labor force and of the variation in employment relationships and in employees' preferences as to how they want to have a voice in and control over their working lives, we also must address regulation issues directly. As with other matters, we urge experimentation with and evaluation of multiple approaches before settling on one or a few approaches that demonstrate superior performance.

Again we have some models to build on. One can be found in the Occupational Safety and Health Administration. Since the early 1980s, OSHA has had a small Voluntary Protection Program available to workplaces that have comprehensive safety-management systems in place and have achieved above-average safety. Among the program's requirements for a comprehensive safety program are that employees have a voice and role in identifying, monitoring, and abating hazards and in other aspects of the program. Work sites that apply for coverage under the program and meet these criteria are then removed from OSHA's general inspection schedule. These agreements need not be limited to a single workplace, and OSHA's Strategic Partnerships Agreements allow consortia of employers to participate. OSHA retains the right (actually the duty) to inspect and investigate fatalities or other serious accidents and the right to respond to employees' complaints. At present, approximately 500 work sites participate in the Voluntary Protection Program. Twenty-eight percent of these are unionized establishments, and therefore the unions present must be joint participants in this effort. To our knowledge there has not been a systematic independent evaluation of this program and so it is premature to argue for its broad expansion. Such an evaluation should be conducted.

The Voluntary Protection Program has elements that might be adapted to other areas of employment policy and regulation. It focuses on outcomes more than specific regulatory standards or on how the parties achieve the goals society has set for a safe workplace. It involves workers, unions, and employers. And it is voluntary and reserved for those workplaces that have built the required local institutional capacity to warrant flexibility and delegation of enforcement responsibilities.[8] These principles could be used to experiment with comparable internal-responsibility systems in other areas of regulation. For example, employers and employees that have comprehensive work/family programs and leave provisions in place could be allowed to meet the broad objectives of the family-leave statute without focusing on specific means for achieving them. Flexibility in how the overtime and compensatory-time provisions of the Fair Labor Standard Act are meshed with variable project schedules, travel requirements, and family responsibilities could also be contemplated. This issue has been debated to an impasse in recent Congressional sessions.

Of course, hours of work and time off for family obligations intersect. If workers and employers were to be encouraged to discuss these matters together at the workplace, a number of creative innovations might emerge that would not be possible if hours of work and time off for family obligations remained subject to separate rules and enforcement regimes.

Experimenting with and Evaluating Alternative Dispute-Resolution Systems

Experimentation is also underway in regard to how disputes involving statutory rights are enforced and adjudicated. The federal Equal Employment Opportunity Commission and the equivalent state agencies are experimenting with alternative dispute-resolution processes on a voluntary basis. This experimentation is not without controversy. Some fear that the use of mediation will provide "second-rate" justice. Others are concerned that it will reduce the deterrent effects of large court awards for egregious violations. Still others worry that the some of the features of these dispute-resolution systems do not meet society's standards of due process.[9] All these issues have been debated in the abstract. Thanks to the EEOC and the Massachusetts Commission Against Discrimination, pilot programs informed by these concerns are in place. The preliminary results are encouraging. Settlements are achieved in about 60 percent of the cases. Satisfaction of the parties is quite high (nearly 90 percent of the claimants and respondents of the EEOC mediation program would use it again); the results seem to approximate what would have been achieved if the case had followed the normal administrative and litigation route, but in a much shorter time and at lower costs to the parties and the agencies; and the EEOC's backlog of 100,000 cases has been cut by more than a half.[10] These preliminary results demonstrate the value of moving from rhetorical debate to concrete results that can be used as a basis for discussions of and experimentation with these options.

Ultimately, it would be preferable to encourage broad-based institutional arrangements that have the capacity to adapt most, if not all, government regulations to fit the particular circumstances of different workplaces. After all, this is what unions and collective bargaining do. The parties set priorities and make tradeoffs concerning the allocation of scarce resources to problems, and therefore they build systems of workplace practices rather than treat specific groups or issues as special cases or separable problems. But we are a long way from having broad-based workplace institutions that are able to take on the full range of responsibilities. Nor are we likely to see the equivalent of a "one-stop" voluntary dispute-resolution venue where a party can take his or her alleged violation and have private or public experts mediate or adjudicate it across statutory boundaries. But these are goals worth working toward. We are likely to get there only if we first build narrower incremental experience and evidence that this approach works in specific areas, then explore how it can be adapted to other areas. But if we were to do so, the goals of flexibility, workplace democracy and voice, and the building of local institutional capacity to address problems closer to their source would all be served.

Summary
This section suggests there are a variety of steps federal agencies can take to make regulations more flexible, more adaptable to the diverse economy, more efficient, and more accessible to those most in need of protection. Most of these steps can be taken without legislation; they require only clear vision on the part of the president, the secretary of labor, and the agencies involved. This vision should be guided by one central idea: that the labor market is now much more diverse and variable than the one that was in place when the New Deal systems were established. In order for the government to achieve the economic and moral

goals we set out in chapter 1, regulatory policy must recognize this diversity. However, we emphasize the importance of openness and flexibility while, at the same time, retaining the view that the federal government, properly structured, remains an essential player in the reconstruction of America's labor-market institutions.

Updating Labor Law

We now enter the troubled waters of labor law. We do so for three important reasons. First, there is general agreement among independent academic experts, business and union leaders, government officials and study commissions, and anyone else who takes the time to examine the evidence that the labor law that grew out of the New Deal no longer achieves the goals it promised the parties and is becoming increasingly irrelevant as a guide to many practices commonly found in workplaces today. Therefore, on its own merits, labor law needs comprehensive updating. Second, many of the other innovations in practice and in the administration and enforcement of regulations discussed in this volume require that labor law be modified if they are to diffuse broadly enough to have a significant impact on the national welfare. Third, the impasse over labor law casts a dark and heavy cloud over the ability of business, labor, and other interested groups to work together in a pragmatic fashion to address other problems. This cloud must be lifted if we are to be open to the experiments and institutional innovations called for in this volume.

Returning to First Principles

The framers of the National Labor Relations Act had the fundamental principles right: Workers should have a choice as to whether to be represented by a union, and where unions have gained recognition labor and management should be free to negotiate terms and conditions of employment that suit their particular needs and circumstances. Though these basic principles are still relevant, the way the law and its court interpretations were molded in the postwar period make it increasingly anachronistic in regard to how work is actually structured and carried out. As a result, the NLRA is not well suited to the current environment.

There is ample evidence that the aforementioned principles are not working for any of the parties. Workers can't gain access to union representation without risking their jobs.[11] The form of representation allowed under the law is too restrictive and is not responsive to what some workers either want or need today. As we discussed in chapter 4, some workers prefer more direct or informal participation; some workers need representation that moves with them across jobs and employers; others want and need the support of community-based organizations that mix advocacy for workers' rights with religious, family, or educational support services. Yet labor law is largely built around assumptions of a fixed work site, majority rule, clear lines of demarcation between manager or supervisor and employee, and prerequisites of majority status. And the law assumes the relationship between employees and employers is inherently adversarial, since unions are only a defensive response to employers that can't be trusted to respect or respond to workers' interests. All these doctrines limit the forms of employee voice and representation that are trying to emerge in different settings—forms that, if allowed to expand, could significantly increase the array of choices open to workers to regain control of their careers and their working lives.

The law doesn't work for employers either, especially those that seek to involve their employees in problem solving and in workplace decision making and management. Although the parts of the law that limit the forms of employee participation are rarely challenged or vigorously enforced, it is clear they are being violated widely. Thus, they neither deter the behavior they were intended to eliminate (formation of company-dominated unions) nor encourage firms to adopt employment practices that have been shown to improve productivity and quality and to be valued by employees.

The current law certainly doesn't work for unions. As we pointed out in chapter 4, notwithstanding the many innovative efforts and increased resources unions are putting into organizing, the returns to date are at best limited. New avenues for recruiting and representing workers and new workable strategies tailored to take advantage of these new options are needed if the next-generation unions and allied associations are to fulfill their roles in society

The current law doesn't work for government agencies either, since it constrains the use of workplace-based "internal-responsibility" systems such as safety and health committees and peer-review committees for grievances. Any effort to give employees and employers more flexibility in deciding how to best comply with workplace regulations is constrained by the law, even though, as we noted above, OSHA and the EEOC are experimenting with these alternatives.

There remains a deep ideological and substantive impasse between business and labor over how to reform or change labor law. Each party has its own preferred legislative and an associated administrative and enforcement agenda. So far, each party has been successful in blocking the other's proposals for reform and therefore has not able to achieve its own. And the latest and most visible effort to find a compromise between the business and labor positions failed. So a fresh approach is needed. We lay out our ideas below, recognizing that it will be some time before they gain enough support to be enacted nationally.

Restoring the Ability to Organize

The starting point in updating labor law must be a restoration of the ability of American workers to decide whether to be represented by a union or an association. Whether workers choose to join traditional unions or unions that offer individual memberships and a broader array of representation and service options (as described in chapter 4 as under the rubric of "next-generation unions") is beside the point. Workers should have the ability to decide whether and in what ways to gain a voice that gives them greater control of their destinies at work.

The debate as to what this restoration will require should focus on how, not whether, to fix the basic problems, which include delays in the processing of union certifications, the risks of being discharged for exercising these rights, and the difficulties encountered in achieving a first contract and launching a new union-management relationship in a constructive fashion. Addressing these issues will inevitably require choosing among alternatives for ensuring prompt certification through elections or other means for demonstrating majority support, strengthening penalties for violating worker rights, and ensuring that, if a majority of workers choose to be represented, they are successful in achieving a first contract by providing mediation, training, and facilitation services (and, if necessary, arbitration of the first agreement). And the same protections against discrimination for being a union or association member should be provided to those who are members of a union that is not a part of a bargaining unit that engages in collective bargaining as we know it today.

Once workers' representation is restored, we come to the second basic question: What kind of collective bargaining structure is most desirable? The basic structure of collective bargaining as it has developed under the NLRA would seem well suited to the requirements of an effective system of workers' representation and negotiation. Indeed, if we were to try to invent a system from scratch it is difficult to believe that we would be able to develop a better one. The basic advantage of the current system is its ability to represent workers' interests and to resolve work problems at the levels at which they arise and to develop solutions adapted to the particular circumstances in which they must be implemented.

Although the basic framework of the NLRA is in many ways ideal, changes in the economy, in the work force, and in industrial organization have rendered many details of the framework anachronistic. One of the most prominent of these details is the sharp line the law attempts to draw between labor and management. The protections of the right to organize do not extend to managers, to the large and rapidly growing class of technical and professional workers who have managerial responsibilities, or to individuals who are in the paid labor force but are excluded from the law because they are classified as independent contractors. Even blue-collar workers who take on managerial responsibilities in self-managing teams could lose their rights to representation if the act were interpreted literally.

This is more than an academic issue. For example, it arises routinely when nurses attempt to organize, since in several NLRB cases and in several court cases it has been ruled that "charge nurses" or others who supervise nursing assistants or other nurses should be excluded from coverage under the NLRA. These managerial and non-managerial distinctions make no sense in today's workplaces. No policy that would exclude more workers from joining unions because they are taking on traditional managerial responsibilities makes any sense. The simplest alternative would be to eliminate the supervisory and managerial exclusion and to allow anyone to join a union or a professional association and gain the protections provided under the NLRA.

Extending the right to be represented by a union or an association to the entire labor force would create a powerful incentive for unions and professional associations to develop the expanded array of services and recruitment and coalition-building strategies envisioned in the network models of union organization and representation discussed in chapter 4. Not all of these organizations would necessarily engage in collective bargaining as we know it today. Whether professional and managerial workers choose to form bargaining units for the purpose of collective bargaining or whether they choose to form more limited organizations and representational modes should again be their choice.

A second area of the law that makes little sense in view of the increased importance of the choice of business strategies, of where the organizational boundaries are placed, and of how new organizational forms or startup operations should be designed is the distinction between "mandatory" and "non-mandatory" subjects of bargaining. This distinction is particularly problematic with respect to the role of information sharing in bargaining and in labor-management partnerships. In view of the increased importance of these issues, employees and their representatives will need access to the information they need in order to make informed judgments on strategic and technical issues. In return, they should be held accountable for protecting the confidentiality of proprietary information. Under the mandatory/non-mandatory doctrine, employers are not required to share this type of information, since it lies outside the scope of mandatory subjects of negotiations. This, at a minimum, should be changed. But should the parties also be allowed to bargain to impasse and to engage in a strike or a lockout over these issues? This is a controversial and difficult question. We believe that society and therefore government would be better off if more of these issues were engaged in a partnership manner, and that is why earlier in this chapter we suggested that the public resources supporting improved labor-management relations be expanded. However, the option for the parties to take a hard stand on these issues should be left open. Simply eliminating the old categories would do this, and perhaps it would spur more parties to develop appropriate consultative forums in which to share sensitive information.

A third anachronism of American labor law is the fact that it is designed for workers with long-term attachments to a well-defined and stable enterprise and a clearly identifiable single employer. It is thus not well adapted to a world in which the boundaries of an enterprise may be constantly shifting through mergers, alliances, and inter-enterprise teams, in which workers move frequently from one enterprise to another, in which the locus of employer responsibility is either ambiguous or shared by two or more firms, or in which the work can be done by traditional employees, by independent contractors, or by leased or temporary employees. Clearly all those who work, no matter how they are classified, should enjoy the same freedom of association and the same protections under other employment laws that are enjoyed by workers in more traditional relationships.

Adapting to the diversity of employment settings and to a more mobile work force will also require shifts in the strategies unions use to recruit and retain members. The industrial-union model generally equates union membership with collective bargaining rights and sees bargaining rights as tied to specific workplaces. This means that every time a worker moves, or every time his job is restructured out of existence, his union membership ceases. To regain union coverage, a worker must once again scale the treacherous terrain of an organizing campaign, with all its delays, conflicts, and risks. This could be avoided if unions and/or associations were to develop new categories of membership and services and if the law were to ensure protection for those who exercise their right to participate in these organizations.

A fourth anachronism is the limits on employees' participation and consultation in the workplace. We noted in chapter 3 that participation and consultation are widespread and expanding. We noted in chapter 4 that employees want to have a voice in new work systems. And we noted earlier in this chapter that the processes that contribute most to improved business performance and those that are most likely to give workers a meaningful voice are precisely those most likely to now be deemed illegal. Moreover, the regulatory agencies that want to experiment with alternative enforcement strategies involving employees are limited in their ability to do so by labor law.

If firms today need these processes, employees want them, and government agencies want to use them more fully, why not simply eliminate all restrictions on employee participation?

As we noted in chapter 4, the real source of controversy is that some firms have used these processes to avoid unionization. This is an inappropriate use of employee participation, and it should continue to be prohibited by labor law. In view of the precarious state of unions in society, we cannot afford to implement any policy that would further undermine their ability to represent the work force in the future. At the same time, firms that are implementing workplace participation and want to take advantage of the internal-responsibility options (described above) for enforcing regulations should not be kept from doing so by firms that violate or disrespect workers' rights.

How to break out of this box is no easy question. Clearly, any experimentation should neither undermine existing union representation nor reduce workers' ability to self-organize if they so choose. We are not sure that we know how to best do these two things, nor do we believe it is impossible to find one or more ways of doing them if we state them as the explicit requirements of any new approaches. So again, careful and informed experimentation and evaluation would appear to be a sensible way to proceed.

There are various ways such experimentation might proceed. For example, OSHA has been consulting with NLRB attorneys in an attempt to clarify how employee participation in the monitoring and enforcement of workplace safety might be achieved without running afoul of current interpretations of the law. If sensible approaches can be fashioned within the current law in this and other regulatory arenas, such experiments should be encouraged and evaluated. Perhaps, over time, the law can evolve as the NLRB interprets it to accommodate current practices.

If in the end the conclusion is that the law limits such experiments, it would be better to specify the minimum standards for employee participation and/or representation that would be needed for a firm or a set of firms in an industry or community to gain the flexibility offered by an internal-responsibility option for administering and enforcing workplace regulations. To be consistent with the basic principles for policy endorsed in this volume, these minimums would have to ensure that workers have the right to choose their own representatives, that they are protected from discrimination or retaliation for exercising their legal rights or for participating in these processes, that they have access to the information and technical advice needed to perform their monitoring functions, and that they have access to a fair and credible system for resolving disputes that might arise.

A third option that could be used in combination with either of the above two approaches, and that is consistent with the experimental strategy we have urged in other areas of policy, would be to allow states or localities to experiment with ways to overcome the anachronisms noted above in the federal statute, as long as the experiments meet or exceed the protections of the federal law. This was the approach that brought the right to organize and to bargain to millions of state and local government employees. In doing so, it produced a number of new ideas for how to resolve contract disputes without resort to strikes—something few labor-relations professionals thought possible. A similar process of experimentation and learning could be put in motion again, and perhaps it would lead to the development and testing of new forms of representation and regulation that would be suited to today's diverse work force and today's employment relationships.

Use of any of these options would essentially set up a two-track labor and employment policy that would link participation, representation, and enforcement of regulations in a way that would be suited to the diversity of work settings found in the present-day economy and would encourage innovation by employers, government, and unions while strengthening the protection of workers in those employment relationships where employers either are not committed or lack the institutional capacity to adapt and enforce workplace regulations.

These are only three ways to experiment with increasing flexibility in regulatory compliance and to build the types of workplace institutions that will be needed if more responsibilities are to be devolved to the parties who understand their work settings the best. Other ways could be generated if a willingness to do so were to be signaled by the relevant policy officials. Such experiments might result in a virtuous cycle of innovation and improvement. Employers would be able to achieve more flexibility in adapting regulations to their specific work environments and business conditions. Workers would have a greater voice in and more control over the things that matter most to them. Unions and professional associations would have opportunities to recruit and serve members in new ways. New incentives and new ways would be created for unions and employers to work together to enhance the quality of labor-management relationships and partnerships, and the objectives of public policy would be achieved at lower costs. But skeptics might envision a vicious cycle in which employers use their new flexibility to undermine independent unions or the voice of workers, workers' rights become harder to enforce, labor standards are compromised, and as a result litigation and tensions among the parties increase. Depending on which scenario results, the appropriate next steps would be clarified. The virtuous cycle would warrant efforts to promote broader diffusion; the vicious cycle would warrant a return to stiffer controls and regulations of inappropriate behavior and increased resources for traditional enforcement procedures.

A Comprehensive Approach

The above discussion should make it clear that piecemeal reforms of labor law are ill-advised and are probably not viable in today's ideologically polarized environment. No single change in the law would be comprehensive enough to close the gap between how work is actually being carried out and the legal doctrines that regulate it. Moreover, single changes inevitably are viewed as favoring one party at the expense of the other and would simply reinforce mistrust and adversarial relations at work. Therefore they are bound to be vigorously opposed by supporters of labor or business in Congress. Nor is some compromise advisable that would give labor a little of what it seeks and business a little of what it seeks. Efforts to fashion such a compromise in the course of the last three decades have failed repeatedly. Instead, a comprehensive overhaul is needed that will address all the anachronistic features of the law in the light of current practice, will restore to workers the rights promised by the original law, and will allow experimentation with new ways to exercise these rights.

Conclusion

Government is obviously a central actor in the labor market. However, in view of the changes which have occurred since the New Deal structures were put into place, it is clear that there is a need to re-think the role of government. In this chapter we have put heavy emphasis on how government can diffuse the local innovations we have described throughout this volume and can stimulate further innovation. We also believe that the increased mobility and risk that characterize the present-day job market require both a strengthening of some institutions (such as unemployment insurance) and a re-thinking of the traditional American strategy of attaching benefits such as health insurance and pensions to employment. As other observers have done, we call for a major commitment to supporting lifelong learning through changes in tax law and through the provision of matching grants to private institutions that will step forward to deliver education and training services to adult workers. We also have made a case for updating the regulations that govern the labor market, including those regarding collective bargaining. A consistent principle guiding all the proposals advanced here is that the ability of the parties closest to the workplace to control their own destinies and to address the challenges they face in the current labor market should be restored.

7

The New Institutions in Action

In the previous chapters we described what we envision as new roles for the major actors in the labor market: firms, unions, new intermediaries, and the government. In this final chapter, to illustrate the power of the approach, we will examine three specific issue areas: low-income labor markets, mobility, and work/family concerns.

Low-Income Labor Markets

The deterioration and the persistence of inequality in income and terms and conditions of employment offered workers at the bottom of the job hierarchy is the most pernicious labor-market problem of our time. Only in 1998, after nearly 7 years of sustained economic expansion and increasingly tight labor markets, did American society see any improvement in incomes and employment opportunities in these markets, and even then many of the families of the working poor remained in poverty. Although strong economic growth and tight labor markets are clearly important starting points for improving opportunities for low-income workers, market forces alone are not likely to reverse this state of affairs. Moreover, a labor-market strategy aimed at addressing the needs of this segment of the economy and society must anticipate future ups and downs in the business cycle and therefore in the contributions and limits of the market. How can the actors in the labor market work together to attack the persistence of low-income labor markets?

Government

The starting point for government policy is macroeconomic policies that maintain high rates of growth and high demand for workers at all levels of the economy, including low-wage workers. This is a necessary condition that, in the long run, will make all the remaining institutional strategies pay off more fully. But it is not sufficient. Other institution-building and regulatory efforts are needed to produce a sustained government strategy for improving the conditions of low-wage workers.

Historically, the major instrument for containing the low-wage labor market in the United States has been the minimum wage. Federal minimum-wage legislation was first introduced in the 1930s. At first, agricultural jobs, much of the services sector, public employment, and small enterprises were exempted. In the postwar period, these exemptions were gradually eliminated, and coverage is now nearly universal. However, the level of the minimum wage relative to the median wage has tended to decline. The decline was quite marked in the 1980s, when wages at the bottom of the market declined sharply.

As a means of raising family income, the minimum wage poses two problems. First, it covers secondary earners (for example, young people) who are not heads of families and whose jobs cannot be judged primarily by the adequacy of the family support that they provide. This problem was much less important in the postwar years, when service jobs were largely excluded, than it has become as coverage has expanded. Second, because the minimum wage increases employers' labor costs, it may lead them to curtail employment opportunities. The strength of this effect is much debated in the scholarly literature.[1] Recent studies suggest that it has been negligible but that it could become important for the range of increases that would be needed to restore the relationship between the minimum wage and the average wage that prevailed in the later 1960s.

One policy instrument that suffers from neither of the above problems is the Earned Income Tax Credit. Introduced into the tax code in 1983, the EITC basically adjusts earnings for family size, providing a subsidy as a percentage of earnings for families below some poverty threshold. It thus compensates for family size in a way in which the minimum wage cannot, and it does not affect employers' incentives to create jobs and hire workers. One of the most impressive achievements of the Clinton administration was to dramatically expand the scope of the EITC. However, when targeted to the most needy, the EITC entails high effective tax rates and creates strong disincentives to increase work effort. These disincentives can be reduced only by reducing the subsidy to families at the bottom of the income scale and increasing them for people who are less needy and arguably not needy at all.

An effective policy for the low-wage sector of the labor market thus requires that the minimum wage and the EITC be used in combination. But here the dispersed nature of government policy making and administration has been a major obstacle. The two policies are administered by different federal agencies and reviewed by different congressional committees. At no point in the policy-making process are their combined effects systematically reviewed, let alone coordinated. This is the first opportunity for national policy makers to clarify their strategy and to coordinate their actions to promote the use of these two policy instruments.

Another problem is that, as the focus of the regulatory process has shifted to higher-wage jobs in the last several decades, enforcement in the low-wage sector has deteriorated. The deterioration has coincided with the increasing dispersion of income. It is difficult to actually demonstrate a causal relationship between these trends, because the level of the minimum wage relative to the median wage also declined in this period. But one of our case studies focused on the Wages and Hours Division of the Department of Labor, where enforcement of the minimum-wage law is lodged, and the deficiencies in the regulatory process were plainly evident. They would presumably become even more apparent if, as we recommend, the level of the minimum were to be restored to its historic relationship to the rest of the wage distribution.

The basic difficulties are as follows.

First, enforcement is based on complaints rather than targeted. This represents a shift in the Wages and Hours Division's enforcement strategy from that of the 1950s and the 1960s, when less than half of its investigations were based on complaints. Targeted investigations increased under the Clinton administration; as late as 1998, however, 71 percent of the investigations were still based on complaints. Targeted investigations force the Wages and Hours Division to think in a systematic way about where violations of the minimum wage are likely to be most severe and how enforcement relates to a broader strategy of eliminating low-wage work. Complaint-based strategies eliminate the need to think in these terms.

Second, the shortcomings of complaint-based investigations are exacerbated by the fact that enforcement of the minimum wage competes within the Department of Labor's Wages and Hours Division with the enforcement of regulations governing higher-wage jobs, for which that division is also responsible. The incentive to complain is dependent on the level of income, since that determines how much a worker can recover. In general, workers are able to recover only the amount of wages to which they were legally entitled, and that only for a maximum of 2 years (3 years if the violation is willful). The incentive to complain is further undermined by the fact that complainants can almost never afford the cost of litigation; their cases are invariably brought by the government, which frequently settles for an injunction against further violations with little or no recovery of past wages. The potential gains are reduced still further for low-wage workers by the fact that their jobs are relatively unstable. Their short job tenure also limits any future gains from a complaint. In fact, the largest potential for gains under the Fair Labor Standards Act is reducing violations of the overtime provisions, which are applicable to all covered workers. The deterrent effect of successful prosecutions in overtime cases in response to complaints is limited by the fact that in the vast majority of cases the employer is required to pay only the wages that should legally have been paid in the first place. Civil penalties for willful violations, introduced in 1989, were not implemented until the early 1990s.

A third complication in regard to application of the minimum-wage laws is a lack of effective cooperation between the Wages and Hours Division and other agencies at the state and local levels (and also at the federal level) that regulate similar jobs. Our interviews with officials of the New England regional office of the Wages and Hours Division and with Massachusetts officials responsible for the enforcement of state labor law revealed that the federal officials were completely misinformed about the substance of the state laws governing the same workplaces for which they were responsible; they were also misinformed about the administrative processes of Massachusetts. Cooperation among federal agencies is also limited, although violations of labor standards tend to cluster in particular firms and industries.

Paradoxically, a fourth difficulty in regard to enforcement of the minimum wage has been perverse collaboration between the

Wages and Hours Division and the Immigration and Naturalization Service that has deterred low-wage workers from cooperating in the enforcement of the minimum wage in their own establishments.

Although there are specific remedies to all of these difficulties, what is really needed is a strategic approach to the low-wage labor market. Leadership by the secretary of labor and the president also is needed.

As an illustration of these points, consider the classic case of the sweatshop. Government audits have shown that inspections of sweatshops uncover violations of the minimum wage, violations of child labor laws, overtime violations, safety and health violations, and other violations.[2] Together these violations promote and reinforce a low-wage production strategy that keeps workers caught in sweatshops from having access to the technologies and the learning opportunities needed to get ahead in today's labor market. Thus, in addition to attacking the specific conditions found in sweatshops in order to protect the human rights of the most marginal workers, various government enforcement agencies should be working together with other enforcement agencies to eliminate sweatshops so that entry-level workers will be able to enter a world of work in which there is chance to share in the opportunities that are open to others in the economy. However, the regulations we are talking about here are dispersed across numerous federal, state, and local agencies. The obvious remedy is a strategy of coordinated enforcement.

Community Groups and Labor-Market Intermediaries

It is clear that an effective strategic approach to low-income labor markets is not likely to grow out of government practice or out of government policy alone. Private actors and institutions must also play prominent roles, and those roles must be complemented and supported by government strategies.

The most imaginative approaches to upgrading low-income labor markets have emerged from the local workers' and community organizations we have described throughout this volume. These organizations are notable not only for how they conceived their approaches strategically but also for how they drew on the knowledge of low-income workers when designing their proposals and for how they combined that knowledge with the expertise of professional experts who understood the broader economic processes constraining the market and guiding its evolution. In earlier chapters we discussed two of the most impressive of these organizations: the Workplace Project on Long Island and the living-wage campaigns, which began in Baltimore and have now been extended to more than 50 cities throughout the United States. Both the Workplace Project and the living-wage campaigns grew out of extensive discussions within an organization and between the organization and outside experts that sought to understand the broad economic context and to develop a holistic strategy. The success of community groups working with unions and other social-welfare advocates in promoting living-wage campaigns in various cities and counties serves as a model for the kinds of innovations that can arise out the deliberative and inclusive processes and coalitions we called for in previous chapters. As they take on these roles, these groups might complement the approach called for by government agencies. Their scope of attention should be the full array of production, technology, and organizational strategies that either separate low-wage workers from opportunities to advance in the new economy or link them to those opportunities. Moreover, these groups might begin to explore ways to gain sufficient standing and expertise to provide training to employee representatives and to serve as technical resources or "one-stop rights centers" for low-wage workers. With government and/or foundation support, experiments could be undertaken to build social networks for families moving from welfare to work—networks that would link child care, income support, job-placement assistance, education, and training in technical and behavioral skills and would represent workers' interests at work. We see such a role as merging with the role of unions at the community level in another blurring of the boundary between a "next-generation union" and a community group.

Unions

One of the most important contributions of the American labor movement from the 1930s through much of the postwar period was their success in upgrading the working conditions and living standards of the "unskilled" or "semi-skilled" production workers in the manufacturing sector. That so many auto workers, steel workers, and other workers moved their families into the middle class was no accident of market forces. Econometric studies drawing on national, industry, and company data sets have consistently demonstrated that unions have improved the wages and benefits of workers in entry-level or lower-level jobs and thereby reduced income differentials.[3] Moreover, by negotiating rules governing access to training and internal job ladders (in addition to providing opportunities to take leadership positions in the labor movement), unions helped integrate low-wage workers into the opportunities for upward mobility in the internal labor markets of the time. Therefore, the revival and rebuilding of unions and collective bargaining we have called for in this volume should be seen as an integral part of a national strategy for addressing both the income and the opportunities that can be created in today's low-income labor markets. However, the strategies unions use to achieve these goals will have to be more varied than in the past, insofar as many low-income workers are scattered in non-standard job settings, many come from immigrant, racial-minority, and cultural-minority communities, and many lack basic language, social, and behavioral skills needed to succeed in the labor market. This is one of the reasons we have suggested that unions and community groups work closely together in a variety of political and organizing efforts. Clearly, for low-income workers to have strong union partners at the community level is an essential component of a concerted strategy for upgrading their jobs and their earnings.

Firms

Like their union counterparts, large integrated firms were important portals of entry and ladders of upward mobility for low-wage workers in the industrial era. If the landscape of the future is to be dominated by knowledge workers and by slimmed-down firms focusing on core competencies, large segments of low-wage workers will be cut off from this option for upward mobility. What then is the role of firms in a concerted strategy for addressing the needs of these workers?

Clearly it is an overstatement to say that large employers now employ only knowledge workers, particularly in regard to large service-sector firms and organizations. Health care, hospitality, information services, financial services, and other service-industry employers will continue to employ large numbers of entry-level workers. Thus, working to create the same internal-labor-market structures for upward mobility via unions, as was illustrated in the San Francisco hotel example in chapter 3, is a classic example of what can be done. But society is also beginning to insist that firms that outsource low-wage work to suppliers and vendors (in the United States or abroad) not be absolved of their responsibilities to see to it that the individuals who do the work are treated fairly and are paid living wages. "No sweat" campaigns at universities around the United States have raised the consciousness of students and of the persons responsible for licensing university products. The public pressures placed on domestic consumer-products firms to work with employees'-rights groups to monitor work conditions in overseas contractor operations are further examples of the growing recognition that firms should be held accountable for the services they purchase and for the work conditions of those they employ directly. Holding firms accountable in this way should be a part of a concerted strategy for upgrading the incomes and opportunities of low-wage workers.

From this brief overview, it is clear that attacking the problem of low-wage jobs and incomes is indeed possible. But a concerted, coordinated effort will be required—it cannot be done in a centralized fashion by some single overarching "actor." There will have to be national and local efforts by various parties, all taking their responsibilities seriously. The institutional structure and the roles for various actors outlined in this volume can open the door.

Mobility

The increased mobility of workers requires significant rethinking of how responsibilities are distributed and shared among the various actors in the labor markets of the future. Exit options and strategies will become more salient, complementing (but not substituting for) voice within any workplace. This is especially likely to be the case for highly educated and skilled professionals and technical workers whose labor-market power and career security depend on their keeping their skills and social networks current over their careers.

We open our discussion of these responsibilities with labor-market intermediaries, community groups, and unions both because we want to highlight their increased importance in these labor markets and because we foresee their roles crossing and their identities blurring. These actors will have to work together more effectively at the level of the local labor market, where most mobility occurs.

Intermediaries, Community Groups, and Unions

There are real gains in economic efficiency to be achieved by organizing job-to-job movement more effectively. By one estimate, independent contractors spend nearly a quarter of their time searching for and landing their next project opportunity.[4] Making this search process more efficient could produce substantial gains in national productivity and in personal incomes. Unions, community groups, educational institutions, temporary-help firms, specialized "headhunters" and consultants, and the enterprises themselves are all involved in creating new arrangements to organize the movement of workers between firms and to provide the associated recruitment, screening, and training services that enterprises used to provide for themselves. In a sense, this is the frontier of the new institutional arrangements.

A host of institutions are emerging to serve the higher end of the labor market. A group of human-resources professionals we met with recently estimated that they can find (and are solicited by) more than 100 Internet-based job-posting and job-matching services. Yet these professionals were quick to point out that most of these services provide only what labor-market scholars of the past called "extensive" (as opposed to "intensive") information on potential applicants.[5] That is, only a few of these services provide enough information for more than preliminary screening. Getting intensive information on professional credibility and reliability, depth of experience, and skill with specific technologies still required more traditional recruitment efforts. Thus, institutions that use the Internet and related communications tools to expand the pool of applicants available *and* that can go the next step of certifying the reliability and the competence of potential candidates would add real value to the efficiency of job matching.

Achieving this will require the creation ongoing social networks whose custodians or facilitators can vouch for the people they refer and can use the data they receive from employers to provide training in the skills that are in the greatest demand. That is essentially what craft unions and professional associations do.

In a new experiment aimed at playing the role just mentioned, the Communication Workers of America have set up a program to train and place military veterans. One of the firms it supplies in this fashion is Cisco Systems. Cisco also has its own "Cisco Academy" program, in which it works with schools to educate and train people in the technologies and standards it needs. Cisco and the CWA are now planning a new experiment that would link the two initiatives.

Assuming similar functions and providing similar services could be a key to the revival and growth of other professional unions and associations. If they do not do this, the void will be filled by for-profit organizations whose primarily allegiances will be (as it is for other temporary-help firms) to the employers they serve. This is not necessarily a bad thing; history tells us that there are serious dysfunctional consequences when any organization gains a monopoly over the labor supply for an occupation. But a mix of institutions that cover the full spectrum from organizations—with some whose mission is to serve and advocate workers' interests, some that are more oriented toward business concerns, and others that position themselves in between—would be the most healthy option for society.

Intermediaries such as those just discussed are not required only at the high end of the job market. Recall from chapter 4 how the Service Employees International Union took on the responsibility of matching home-care workers with potential clients. These workers benefit greatly from the SEIU's transportation and patient-referral services. The union has now assumed a position in the labor market in which it can either provide such services itself or bargaining with the county to do so. This example illustrates the power and the leverage that are available to an institution that can place itself in a mediating position at the nodes where workers and enterprises connect.

Unions and professional associations also should develop new ways to represent contingent workers and to provide them with a voice in the workplace. And it is impossible to imagine a structure of regulatory devolution without strong representative institutions for contingent workers. The examples of health and safety and of sexual harassment discussed below in relation to the outsourcing of supervision illustrate this point.

Firms

As mobility becomes more common in the labor market, it becomes increasingly difficult to identify how various organizations should assume or share the responsibilities typically assigned to the employer for meeting obligations imposed by law. How, for example, is responsibility for meeting legal obligations distributed between a firm purchasing the services of contract laborers and an intermediary that supplies the laborers? This question revolves around the definition of "employer," and that definition varies from one piece of legislation to another in the complex legal framework that governs the work relationship. One important question concerns who supervises the work and who is responsible for the range of personnel functions such as payroll, recruitment, screening, training, and promotion. In most of the emergent structures, it would appear, employers are seeking to retain supervisory responsibility and some control of training and promotion but to relinquish the rest of their traditional employment functions to contractors. The courts have been increasingly reluctant to have it both ways, and this has created a trend toward outsourcing of supervisory functions. We have a major concern about this development. It is antithetical to the nature of the work process. Most of the work that actually occurs in a particular establishment is a social enterprise. Furthermore, many of the obligations imposed by regulation cannot be met effectively (and some cannot be met at all) if the social nature of the enterprise is not recognized and managed. Managing health and safety in chemical plants rests on a coordinated strategy involving the design of production and maintenance systems, the flow of communication across workers, the way in which workers are trained to relate to one another, and the supervision of these interconnected activities. When maintenance is outsourced to a contractor, this integration among the workers and within the productive process often breaks down. Studies have shown that accidents increase when that happens.[6] Similarly, in a very different area—sexual harassment—it is impossible to maintain the "non-hostile" environment required by law if supervisors in an enterprise use one standard for themselves and another for their workers. The attempt to build a wall between the realm of the contractor and the realm of the intermediary makes it difficult to comply with the spirit of the law or to implement it in an efficient and effective way. This is a very unsettled area of practice and law, and its resolution will require both action by government and continued experimentation and evaluation by the parties to enhance the quality of coordination across these organizational boundaries.

Government

The above discussion suggests one important role for government: to consolidate the multiple (at last count as many as 20) definitions used by various agencies to define terms such as "employee" and "employer." The principle here is that *all* who are in the paid labor force are workers and should be so defined and covered under the protections society affords "workers." The opportunity for employers to avoid taking responsibility for

Social Security, unemployment insurance, and other obligations by just redefining workers as independent contractors is both morally unacceptable and costly to society. It also makes enforcement and compliance difficult, since who the Internal Revenue Service deems an employee for purposes of Social Security and for other tax purposes can be different from who Occupation Safety and Health Administration or the Wage and Hour Administration deems an employee in enforcement programs. Once the definition of "employee" is expanded in this way, the complex question as to which employer is responsible (or shares responsibility) for enforcing workplace standards can be addressed more sensibly. These are complex matters, and their detailed resolution lies well beyond the scope of our analysis. However, the responsibility of government leaders is to get on with the task.

As we explained earlier, the federal government must get on with the task of increasing the portability of benefits and pensions and should move incrementally down the path of separating benefit coverage from employment status. Indeed, addressing how to modify our approach to benefits is only the beginning of a complete analysis of how to modify labor-market policies such as unemployment insurance, family benefits (current and future), and all other government-conferred benefits that are now tied to hours worked for a specific employer or to continuous hours in the labor market within a specified period (e.g., a year). These decision rules for financing benefits all reflect the old, stable labor markets in which workers were tied to single employers by full-time jobs. The flexibility that workers and firms need in view of today's family pressures, customer requirements, and labor markets all call for a careful review and for a comprehensive revision of the funding and eligibility rules for these programs. Owing to the number of people and organizations invested in the existing system, migrating from a single firm to some alternative way of funding and delivering labor-market services and income security benefits will be a long and incremental process.

The challenges posed by the need to foster mobility for larger segments of the working population illustrate how the various institutional actors need to work together in new ways. Our final example, family and work, will demonstrate this interdependence even more vividly and will further show that the institutions governing work should be linked more fully to institutions in other parts of civil society and to social policy.

Family and Work

Labor-market institutions and community organizations that focus on family and child care and development are only beginning to explore in a systematic fashion how to address the increasing interdependence between family responsibilities and work responsibilities. The first task in this area is to end the separation between these two domains of social policy and analysis. We can already begin to see the outlines of how a concerted strategy to link the efforts of individual firms, community groups, and unions with public policy initiatives might address the family and work issues for larger segments of the work force than any of those actors now reach.

Firms
Consider the evidence on the distribution and the functioning of firm-initiated family-friendly policies. First, these policies are designed, appropriately, to make it easier for workers to meet their family obligations while allowing them to do their jobs. Firms start from the question of how family-friendly policies will contribute to business performance. This is as it should be. Just like the experience with high-performance or knowledge-based work systems described in chapter 3, once firms began to

see family-friendly policies as central to business competitiveness the adoption and the diffusion of such policies increased. Indeed, the patterns of adoption appear to be similar for both sets of practices.[7] Second, these benefits are often only conferred on higher-level employees, who have more labor-market power than lower-level employees and who are in shorter supply. Third, as we noted in earlier chapters, a growing body of evidence suggests that actual take-up and use of these firm-provided policies depends on the extent to which employees have a voice in controlling the use of their schedules and on the extent to which the culture of the workplace encourages their use. Thus, employer-provided policies are the starting point for a coordinated labor-market strategy addressing work and family concerns. But gaining the full payoff to these policies will require collective, collaborative participation by front-line workers and supervisors.

Community Groups and Unions

If firm-provided benefits and services are not to increase inequality in the job hierarchy, they will have to be complemented by efforts of unions, community groups, and government. Unions have a tremendous opportunity here. The growing numbers of young parents in unions and in the pool of potential union members are natural clienteles for next-generation unions. Some unions are already quite actively negotiating benefits and organizing or coordinating services in this arena, a classic case being the Harvard Clerical and Technical Workers Union.

We mentioned in chapter 5 that a number of for-profit and non-profit family and work intermediaries have emerged in recent years. Most of these, like the firms they see as their clients, serve the upper end of the labor market. They are making important contributions to publicizing the best practices of firms, assessing firm-based programs, and working with work/family professionals within firms to advocate for these programs. Thus, they are helping to move family and work issues to center stage in the corporate world. However, few of these intermediaries serve the needs of low-income workers and families. Yet low-wage working families have the greatest need for assistance. Meeting family needs is tightly coupled with the other strategies discussed above for improving the wages, benefits, and other labor-market experiences of low-wage workers.

Government

More than any other set of issues, work and family issues illustrate the basic points we have made throughout this volume as to how government policy should proceed in this relatively uncharted territory. Government must be informed by what firms and other private institutions are doing and should design policies that complement those efforts. Instead of simply telling state governments that they are free to use their unemployment-compensation funds to provide paid leave, the federal government might do well to actively promote state and local experimentation with flexible ways to complement firm-provided benefits and policies. For their part, employers should avoid reacting in knee-jerk fashion to any ideas of additional government policy in this arena and should begin to engage in a dialogue with policy makers and with the women's groups and labor groups that are advocating expanded benefits on the subject of how to expand benefits in the most flexible and mutually beneficial manner. There is a real danger of mindless opposition. For example, the Society for Human Resource Management (the major organization serving the human-resources profession) routinely leads the fight against any expansion of the Family and Medical Leave Act, while the National Organization for Families and Women leads the efforts to promote such expansion. The spokeswomen for these two organizations often debate in public policy forums and in the media. The battle lines are being drawn in a way that will replicate the business/labor divide that created a sustained impasse over labor policy.

There must be, and we believe can be, a better way if the parties with interests in this issue engage in a dialogue on how to proceed. For example, we recently posed the following hypothetical question to a gathering of human-resources managers and consultants: "Assume there will be some form of paid leave enacted by government sometime in the future. How would you shape it to best support and complement and extend rather than conflict with your efforts?" The answer is a good starting point for negotiations with other interested parties: These professionals would prefer a general pooling of funds and banked time off credits that could be drawn on over time to meet a variety of family or other personal needs. In their view, such an approach would avoid divisions within the work force between those with heavy parental or elder-care responsibilities and those with other needs or concerns and would avoid the "one size fits all" aspect of standard regulations and rules. These same professionals took for granted that making such a system work would require some kind of employee input and participation, but they were clear that these participatory processes would be acceptable and would work only if they enhanced cooperation and coordination in the workplace and did not devolve into adversarial processes and relationships. Their response brings us back to the need to invent and experiment with new forms of employee participation that can be sustained in organizations without violating either the basic objectives or the letter of labor law and which promote coordination, cooperation, innovation, and employee influence with regard to important matters affecting workers and their families.

We end this section with a thought experiment. Imagine the possibilities that complementary efforts to address work and family pressures would open up if the new institutional structures, the relationships among them, and the leadership needed to give them direction and energy were in place. Individual firms would continue to do what is in their self-interest by developing family-friendly policies suited to the needs of their particular work force and their particular organizations. Workplace-participation groups or committees would be encouraged and supported to ensure a culture that allows workers to "feel free" to use these policies to better integrate their family and work lives without fear of the consequences for their careers. These committees might be part of an establishment-level representative council responsible for seeing that the objectives of the public policies embodied in the Family and Medical Leave Act and in other statutes are being met, albeit through specific practices or means adapted to fit the situation of the establishment and its work force. Individual firms (especially small ones) might pool their resources and work with community groups and union leaders to ensure the availability of family and child-care services to lower-income workers and their families. Union leaders would be promoting these issues both at collective bargaining tables (where they are the authorized bargaining representatives) and in alliances with community leaders and family advocates. Armed with a knowledge of what these private institutions and market forces are doing in this area, state legislatures and federal policy makers could then take up the question of how to best support and complement what these private actors are doing. Specifically, they would have a better basis for debating proposals such as whether to use the unemployment-insurance system or some other instrument to provide paid leave for family-related reasons.

Final Thoughts

What we have outlined here is, obviously, only one possible vision of how new institutions might work together to attack the three critical challenges facing workers and employers in current labor markets. Other combinations are possible too, depending on the specific policy instruments chosen to bring the energies of the various actors together. What is needed, obviously, is the political support to make this happen.

Although we argue here for a fresh and comprehensive recasting and updating of government policies, it would be naive to expect this to happen overnight. That is not how public policy is made in the United States. Building support for the ideas laid out here will take determined efforts over a long period of time. The deliberative, experimental, and learning processes proposed here must be ongoing and must become normal elements of the process of making employment and labor-market policy. Incremental reforms are easier to achieve and to build on if the key parties know that they will be engaged in an ongoing dialogue guided by a consistent vision and evaluated against clear goals and objectives. Nor is it necessary to envision deliberations occurring in any single forum or "blue ribbon" commission. Instead, dialogue is needed at all levels of the economy discussed here—at the national level, in local communities, in sectors of the economy, and at the transnational level.

If the new roles for government proposed in this chapter are to become realities, the president, the secretary of labor, and the leaders in Congress must have a clear, shared vision of the future of labor policy and must be willing to communicate that vision clearly to the American public. And while unions and business remain central players, new voices must be brought into these deliberations. Little progress is likely to be made on these issues until the American public sees why these issues should be on the national agenda. All Americans have a stake in the future of work. Their voices are essential to transforming labor and employment policy making from back-room special-interest politics to policy making that is shaped by and responsive to the realities of work as they experience it.

Moving to this new institutional structure will require political change and public policy action. There will be such change and such action only if the American public engages these issues and demands they be put on the national agenda. As we were drafting this volume, *Business Week* reported on a poll of the American public done by Louis Harris under the headline "Hey, what about us?" (December 27, 1999). The data in this poll were startling: 75 percent of Americans believed that the benefits of the "new economy" have been distributed unevenly, 69 percent that business was doing a poor or fair job of raising living standards, 61 percent that globalization was helping the United States, 65 percent that globalization was good for American companies and consumers, and 70 percent that globalization was good for developing economies. Only 46 percent saw globalization as creating jobs in the United States. There was broad awareness of the benefits of productivity to the economy: 79 percent agreed that a productivity boom was occurring in the American economy. But when asked about its impact on them, only 34 percent agreed it was increasing their incomes, and only 30 percent that it had enhanced their job security. (Fifty percent recognized it had increased the value of their investments.) Overall, only 53 percent saw the boom as making their lives better. Thus, after nearly 10 years of economic prosperity, nearly half of the Americans surveyed still felt they were not sharing in its benefits, and three-fourths felt that its benefits were not being shared in a way they deemed equitable. Poll data like these should be taken as only one indication and one data point. However, we believe that they signal a larger unease in American society, and that the energy of that unease should channeled into mobilizing the leaders who, in one way or another, will shape the world of work in the future. To catch up with the nature of the work force and with the expectations that workers and their families bring to the labor market, we need new institutions and policies.

Appendix A
Members of Task Force

Eileen Appelbaum	Economic Policy Institute
Elaine Bernard	Harvard University Trade Union Program
Ron Blackwell	AFL-CIO
Margaret Blair	Georgetown University
William Bucknall	United Technologies Corporation
Muzaffar Chishti	UNITE Immigration Project
Dorothy Sue Cobble	Rutgers University
Ernesto Cortes	Industrial Areas Foundation
Ralph Craviso	Lucent Technologies, Inc.
Amy Dean	Working Partnerships USA
Peter Edelman	Georgetown University
Jennifer Gordon	Yale Law School
Sara Horowitz	W. E. Upjohn Institute
Thomas Kochan	Massachusetts Institute of Technology
Joe Laymon	Ford Motor Company
Richard Locke	Massachusetts Institute of Technology
Nancy Mills	AFL-CIO
Paul Osterman	Massachusetts Institute of Technology
Chris Owens	AFL-CIO
Hilary Pennington	Jobs for the Future

Michael Piore	Massachusetts Institute of Technology
Dennis Rocheleau	General Electric
William Spriggs	National Urban League, Inc.
Michael Wald	Stanford University
Janet Zobel	National Urban League, Inc.

Appendix B
Other Participants

Thomas Aleinikoff	Georgetown University Law School
Bernard Anderson	US Department of Labor
Joshua Angrist	Massachusetts Institute of Technology
Regina Austin	University of Pennsylvania Law School
Tom Bailey	Columbia University
Lotte Bailyn	Massachusetts Institute of Technology
Barbara Baran	Corporation for Business, Work and Learning
Stephen Barley	Stanford University
James Baron	Stanford University
Rosemary Batt	Cornell University
Corrine Bendersky	Massachusetts Institute of Technology
Marc Bendick	Bendick & Egan Economic Consultants
Chris Benner	Working Partnerships USA
Michael Bennett	United Auto Workers
Annette Bernhardt	Institute on Education and the Economy
Jared Bernstein	Economic Policy Institute
Ann Bookman	Massachusetts Institute of Technology
Forrest Briscoe	Massachusetts Institute of Technology
Judson Broome	Instron Corporation

Clair Brown	University of California, Berkeley
Françoise Carré	Radcliffe Public Policy Institute
Susan Cass	Massachusetts Institute of Technology
Kathleen Christensen	Alfred P. Sloan Foundation
Susan Christopherson	Cornell University
Robert Clark	North Carolina State University
Rachael Cobb	Massachusetts Institute of Technology
Joshua Cohen	Massachusetts Institute of Technology
John Colborn	Ford Foundation
Grace Colman	Lucent Technologies, Inc.
Charles Darrah	San Jose State University
Mary Davidson	Rutgers University School of Social Work
Gerald Davis	University of Michigan Business School
Peter Doeringer	Boston University
Susan Eaton	Harvard University
Adrienne Eaton	Rutgers University
Enid Eckstein	AFL-CIO
Fred Feinstein	National Labor Relations Board
Aaron Feuerstein	Malden Mills
Hector Figueroa	Service Employees International Union
Janice Fine	Massachusetts Institute of Technology and Northeast Action
Robert Gibbons	Massachusetts Institute of Technology
Jeff Grabelsky	Cornell University School of Industrial and Labor Relations
Michael Grace	Communication Workers of America
W. Norton Grubb	University of California, Berkeley
Brett Hammond	TIAA-CREF
William Hanson	Massachusetts Institute of Technology

Heidi Hartmann	Institute for Women's Policy Research
Charles Heckscher	Rutgers University
Susan Helper	National Labor Relations Board and Case Western Reserve University
Bruce Herman	AFL-CIO Working for America Institute
Stephen Herzenberg	Keystone Research Center
Jonathan Hiatt	AFL-CIO
William Hobgood	UAL Corporation
Susan Houseman	W. E. Upjohn Institute
Maria Iannozzi	Iannozzi Communications
Paul Johnston	Citizenship Project
Lewis Kaden	Davis, Polk and Wardwell
Harry Katz	Cornell University
Richard Kazis	Jobs for the Future
Jen Kern	ACORN (Association of Community Organizations for Reform Now)
Steve Kest	ACORN
Deborah Kolk	Simmons College
Alan Krueger	Princeton University
Gideon Kunda	Stanford University
Renee Landers	Ropes & Gray
Jonathan Lange	Industrial Areas Foundation
Mary Lassen	Women's Educational and Industrial Union
Donna Lenhoff	National Partnership for Women and Families
Robert Lerman	Urban Institute
Frank Levy	Massachusetts Institute of Technology
Lance Lindblom	Ford Foundation
Gary Loveman	Harrah's Entertainment, Inc.

Jonathan Low	Ernst & Young
Lisa Lynch	Tufts University
Christopher Mackin	Ownership Associates, Inc.
Lynelle Mahon	1199 Child Care Fund
Mara Manus	Ford Foundation
Jane McAlevey	Stamford Organizing Project
Katherine McFate	Rockefeller Foundation
Richard McGahey	US Department of Labor
Robert McKersie	Massachusetts Institute of Technology
Eliseo Medina	Service Employees International Union
Richard Monczka	UAW-GM Center for Human Resources
Maureen O'Connor	Stetson University College of Law
Maria Onpiveros	Golden Gate University
Gail Pesyna	Alfred P. Sloan Foundation
Maureen Quinn	Manpower, Inc.
Paula Rayman	Radcliffe Public Policy Institute
Kris Rondeau	Harvard Union of Clerical and Technical Workers
Mary Rowe	Massachusetts Institute of Technology
Saul Rubinstein	Rutgers University
Sean Safford	Massachusetts Institute of Technology
AnnaLee Saxenian	University of California, Berkeley
Maureen Scully	Simmons College
Jay Siegel	John F. Kennedy School of Government
Theda Skocpol	Harvard University
Sue Smock	US Department of Labor
William Spring	Federal Reserve Bank of Boston
Daphne Taras	University of Calgary
Judith Tendler	Massachusetts Institute of Technology

Chris Tilly	University of Massachusetts, Lowell
Robert Tobias	National Treasury Employees Union
Liem Tran	STRIVE/Boston Employment Service, Inc.
Weezie Waldstein	AFL-CIO Working for America Institute
Jeanne Wallace	Malden Mills
Howard Wial	Keystone Research Center
Lynn Williams	United Steelworkers

Notes

Chapter 1

1. For a useful discussion of changing economic structures, see Stephen Herzenberg, John Alic, and Howard Wial, *New Rules for a New Economy: Employment and Opportunity in Postindustrial America* (ILR Press, 1998).

2. AnnaLee Saxenian, Silicon Valley's New Immigrant Entrepreneurs: Skills, Networks and Careers (Working Paper 05, MIT Task Force on Reconstructing America's Labor Market Institutions, 1999).

3. See the preface.

4. Theresa Welbourne and Linda Cyr, "The Human Resource Executive in Initial Public Offerings," *Academy of Management Journal* 42 (1999): 616–629; M. Diane Burton and Charles O'Reilly, The Impact of High Commitment Values and Practices on Technology Start-Ups (Working Paper, MIT Sloan School of Management, 2000).

5. Joshua Cohen and Joel Rogers, *Associations and Democracy* (Verso, 1995).

6. Theda Skocpol, *Protecting Soldiers and Mothers: The Political Origins of Social Policy in the United States* (Harvard University Press, 1992).

7. Paul Osterman and Brenda Lautsch, Project QUEST: A Report to the Ford Foundation, 1997.

Chapter 2

1. Anthony Freeman, "ILO Labor Standards and US Compliance," *Perspectives on Work* 3, no. 1 (1999): 26–31.

2. Families and the Labor Market, 1969–1999: Analyzing the "Time Crunch" (White Paper, US Council of Economic Advisors, 1999), p. 3.

3. Ibid., p. 8.

4. US Department of Labor, Futurework—Trends and Challenges for Work in the 21st Century (1999) (http://www.dol.gov/dol/asp/public/futurework/).

5. Ibid., p. 33.

6. Ibid., p. 3.

7. Paul Osterman, "How Common Is Workplace Transformation and Who Adopts It?" *Industrial and Labor Relations Review* 47 (1994), no. 2: 173–187.

8. Work and Family Benefits Provided by Major US Employers in 1996 (Hewitt Associates, 1997).

9. Susan Eaton, Work-Family Integration in Biotechnology: Implications for Firms and Employees (Ph.D. dissertation, MIT Sloan School, 2000); Françoise Carré et al., Professional Pathways: Examining Work, Family and Community in the Biotechnology Industry (Report to Alfred P. Sloan Foundation, 1999); Mindy Fried, *Taking Time* (Temple University Press, 1998).

10. Rosemary Batt, Alex Colvin, and Jeffrey Keefe, Workplace Flexibility, Work-Family Integration, and Employee Turnover (Working Paper, Cornell University School of Industrial and Labor Relations, 2000).

11. Paul Osterman, *Securing Prosperity: The American Labor Market: How It Has Changed and What to Do about It* (Princeton University Press, 1999), pp. 41–43.

12. Staffing Industry Analysts, *Staffing Industry Reports* 7 (1997), no. 14, p. 10.

13. Rosemary Batt, Performance and Welfare Effects of Work Restructuring: Evidence From Telecommunications Services (Ph.D. dissertation, MIT Sloan School of Management, 1995).

14. The median duration of a temporary job (i.e., an assignment from a temporary-help firm) was 3 months; the median duration of an on-payroll contingent job was 9 months. There are twice as many temporary jobs as contingent jobs.

15. AnnaLee Saxenian, Silicon Valley's New Immigrant Entrepreneurs: Skills, Networks, and Careers (Working Paper 05, MIT Task Force on Reconstructing America's Labor Market Institutions, 1999), p. 1. See also Saxenian, *Silicon Valley's New Immigrant Entrepreneurs* (Public Policy Institute of California, 1999).

16. Gideon Kunda, Stephen Barley, and James Evans, Why Do Contractors Contract? The Theory and Reality of High End Contingent Labor (Working Paper 04, MIT Task Force on Reconstructing America's Labor Market Institutions, 1999), pp. 33–34.

17. Ibid., p. 37.

18. Saxenian, Silicon Valley's New Immigrant Entrepreneurs.

19. Ibid., p. 36.

20. For a detailed discussion of the data on dislocation, see Osterman, *Securing Prosperity*, pp. 78–84.

21. Cynthia Gustafson, Job Displacement and Mobility of Younger Workers (Working Paper 8, Center for Labor Economics, University of California, Berkeley, 1998).

22. Osterman, *Securing Prosperity*, p. 86.

23. C. N. Darrah, Temping at the Lower End: An Incomplete View from Silicon Valley (Working Paper 10, MIT Task Force on Reconstructing America's Labor Market Institutions, 1999), p. 7.

24. Ibid. p. 18.

25. These conclusions hold after more sophisticated controls, such as a regression equation estimating an individual's hourly wage as a function of a long list of personal characteristics and a variable that measures whether or not the individual is in a contingent job.

26. David Autor, Larry Katz, and Alan Krueger, "Computing Inequality: Have Computers Changed the Labor Market?" *Quarterly Journal of Economics* 113 (November 1998): 1245–1279; Eli Berman, John Bound, and Zvi Griliches, "Changes in the Demand for Skilled Labor within US Manufacturing: Evidence from the Annual Survey of Manufacturers," *Quarterly Journal of Economics* 109, no. 2 (1994): 367–397; Frank Levy and Richard Murnane, "With What Skills Are Computers a Complement?" *American Economic Review* 86 (1996), no. 2 (Papers and Proceedings): 258–262; Frank Levy, Anne Beamish, Richard Murnane, and David Autor, Computerization and Skills: Examples from a Car Dealership (Working Paper, IWER Seminar Series, 2000).

27. Paul Osterman, "Skill, Training, and Work Organization in American Establishments," *Industrial Relations* 34 (1995), no. 2: 125–146; Lisa Lynch and Sandra Black, What's Driving the New Economy: The Benefits of Workplace Innovation (Working Paper, IWER Seminar Series, 1999); Sandra Black and Lisa Lynch, How to

Compete: The Impact of Workplace Practices and Information Technology on Productivity (Working Paper 6120, National Bureau of Economic Research, 1997).

28. eWorking to the Future: Labor Requirements of the New Economy (conference at MIT Sloan School of Management, 2000).

29. For a discussion of these causes of union decline, see the various articles by Henry Farber, Richard Freeman, Janice Klein and David Wanger, and Anil Verma and Thomas Kochan in *Challenges and Choices Facing American Labor*, ed. T. Kochan (MIT Press, 1985). For more recent analyses of the causes of union decline in the United States and other countries, see *Employee Representation*, ed. B. Kaufman and M. Kleiner (Industrial Relations Research Association, 1994) or *World Labour Report: Industrial Relations, Democracy, and Social Stability* (International Labour Organization, 1997).

30. Francis Blau and Larry Kahn, "International Differences in Male Wage Inequality: Institutions versus Market Forces," Journal *of Political Economy* 104 (August 1996): 791–837; David Card, Falling Union Membership and Rising Wage Inequality: What's the Connection? (Working Paper 6520, National Bureau of Economic Research, 1998); John DiNardo, Nicole Fortin, and Thomas Lemieux, "Labor Market Institutions and the Distribution of Wages, 1973–1992: A Semi-Parametric Approach," *Econometrica* 64 (1996), no. 5: 1001–1044; Richard Freeman and James Medoff, *What Do Unions Do?* (Basic Books, 1984).

31. John Dunlop, "The Limits of Legal Compulsion," *Labor Law Journal* 27 (1976), no. 2: 67–74.

32. For a review of this history, see John Dunlop and Arnold Zack, *Arbitration and Mediation of Employment Disputes* (Jossey-Bass, 1997).

33. Fact Finding Report of the Commission on Worker Management Relations (US Departments of Commerce and Labor, 1994).

34. Final Report and Recommendations of the Commission on the Future of Worker Management Relations. (US Departments of Commerce and Labor, 1994), p. 44.

35. Interview, EEOC staff, June 2000.

36. Louis Uchitelle, "INS Is Looking the Other Way as Illegal Immigrants Fill Jobs," *New York Times*, March 9, 2000.

37. Maria Echaveste and Karen Nussbaum, "Viewpoints: 96 Cents an Hour: The Sweatshop is Reborn," *New York Times*, August 6, 1994.

38. Howard Wial, Minimum-Wage Enforcement and the Low-Wage Labor Market (Working Paper 11, MIT Task Force on Reconstructing America's Labor Market Institutions, 1999). (Wial also reports that the majority of these cases involve inadvertent and relatively minor violations.)

39. This is calculated from the March 1999 Current Population Survey. The data are arrived at by summing the number of people of ages 25–64 who worked full time and full year and earned less than $17,499 a year. The $8.50 figure is based on the assumption that a full time, full year worker works 2080 hours a year. For the data, see http://ferret.bls.census/gov/macro/031999/perinc/new06_ooo.htm.

40. Osterman, "Skill, Training, and Work Organization in American Establishments."

41. Daniel McMurrer, Mark Condon, and Isabel Sawhill, *Intergenerational Mobility in the United States* (Urban Institute, 1997).

42. Peter Gottschalk, "Inequality, Income Growth, and Mobility: The Basic Facts," Journal *of Economic Perspectives* 11 (1997), spring: 21–40.

43. J. Bond, E. Galinsky, and J. Swanberg, *The 1997 National Study of the Changing Workforce* (Families and Work Institute, 1998).

44. Charles Heckscher found that many middle managers in downsizing American firms retained loyalty toward their employer even when they knew the organization was likely to let them go (Heckscher, *White-Collar Blues*, Basic Books, 1995).

45. David Levine, Dale Belman, Gary Charness, Erica Groshen, and K. O'Shaughnessy, *Changes in Careers and Wage Structures at Large American Employers* (W. E. Upjohn Institute for Employment Research, forthcoming).

Chapter 3

1. Adolf Berle and Gardiner Means, *Modern Corporation and Private Property* (Macmillan, 1933).

2. Sanford Jacoby, *Modern Manors: Welfare Capitalism since the New Deal* (Princeton University Press, 1997).

3. Gregory Acs and Eugene Steuerle, "The Corporation as a Dispenser of Welfare and Security," in *The American Corporation Today*, ed. C. Kaysen (Oxford University Press, 1996).

4. Marina v. N. Whitman, *New World, New Rules* (Harvard Business School Press, 1999), p. 45.

5. Charles Brown and James Medoff, The Employer Size Wage Effect (Working Paper 287, National Bureau of Economic Research, 1989).

6. Geoffrey Garrett, *Partisan Politics in the Global Economy* (Cambridge University Press, 1998), p. 51.

7. Ibid., p. 53.

8. Geoffrey Garrett, "Globalization and Government Spending around the World," *Studies in Comparative and International Development* 35 (2001), no. 4.

9. Garrett, *Partisan Politics in the Global Economy*, p. 54.

10. Richard Herring and Robert Litan, *Financial Regulation in the Global Economy* (Brookings Institution, 1995), pp. 26–27.

11. Helen Milner and Robert Keohane, "Internationalization and Domestic Politics: An Introduction," in *Internationalization and Domestic Politics*, ed. Keohane and Milner (Cambridge University Press, 1996), p. 12.

12. Rosemary Batt, "Work Organization, Technology, and Performance in Customer Service and Sales," *Industrial and Labor Relations Review* 52 (1999), July: 539–564.

13. Larry Hunter, Annette Bernhardt, Katherine Huges, and Eva Skuratowicz, "It's Not Just ATMs: Technology, Firm Strategies, Jobs, and Earnings in Retail Banking," *Industrial and Labor Relations Review* 54 (2001), no. 2: 402–424.

14. Michael Belzer, *Sweatshops on Wheels* (University of Michigan, 2000).

15. Harry Katz and Owen Darbishire, *Converging Divergences* (ILR Press, 2000), pp. 57–58.

16. Michael Useem, *Investor Capitalism* (Basic Books, 1996).

17. Interview.

18. Theresa Wellbourne and Linda Cyr, "The Human Resource Executive Effect in Initial Public Offerings," Academy *of Management Journal* 42 (1999): 616–629.

19. M. Diane Burton and Charles O'Reilly, The Impact of High Commitment Values and Practices on High Technology Start Ups (Working Paper, MIT Sloan School of Management, 2000).

20. For a thorough analysis of Kodak's employment and community relations history, see Jacoby, *Modern Manors*.

21. Michael Santoli, "Kodak's New Colors," *Barrons*, August 24, 1998, p. 25.

22. For a review of Kodak through the 1980s and the 1990s, see Alecia Swasy, *Changing Focus: Kodak and the Battle to Save a Great American Company* (Random House, 1997).

23. Jody Hoffer Gittell, "Organizing Work to Support Relational Co-ordination," *International Journal of Human Resource Management* 11 (2000), no. 3: 517–539; Gittell, "Paradox of Coordination and Control," *California Management Review* 42 (2000), no. 3, p. 101.

24. Gittell, "Organizing Work to Support Relational Co-ordination" and "Paradox of Coordination and Control."

25. Robert Oakeshott, Majority Employee Ownership at United Airlines: Evidence of Big Wins for Both Jobs and Investors (case study commissioned by Partnership Research Ltd. and Unit Trust Bank PLC, London, July 1997).

26. For a review of the various estimates, see Paul Osterman, "Work Organization in an Era of Restructuring: Trends in Diffusion and Impacts on Employee Welfare," *Industrial and Labor Relations Review* 53 (2000), no. 2: 179–196.

27. Paul Osterman, "How Common Is Workplace Transformation and How Can We Explain Who Does It?" *Industrial and Labor Relations Review* 47, no. 2 (1994): 175–188.

28. Osterman, "Work Organization in an Era of Restructuring."

29. John MacDuffie, "Human Resource Bundling and Manufacturing Performance: Organizational Logic and Flexible Production Systems in the World Automobile Industry," *Industrial and Labor Relations Review* 48 (1995), no. 2: 197–221.

30. Casey Ichniowski, Katherine Shaw, and Giovanna Prennushi, "The Impact of Human Resource Practices on Productivity," *American Economic Review* 87, no. 3 (1997): 291–313.

31. Batt, *Performance and Welfare Effects of Work Restructuring*.

32. Peter Berg, Eileen Appelbaum, Thomas Bailey, and Arne Kalleberg, "The Performance Effects of Modular Production in the Apparel Industry," *Industrial Relations* 35 (1995), no. 3: 356–374.

33. John Delery and D. Harold Doty, "Modes of Theorizing in Strategic Human Resource Management: Tests of Universalistic, Contingency, and Configurational Performance," *Academy of Management Journal* 39 (1996): 802–835.

34. Joel Cutcher-Gershenfeld, "The Impact on Economic Performance of a Transformation in Workplace Relations," *Industrial and Labor Relations Review* 44 (1991): 241–260.

35. See e.g. Eileen Appelbaum, Thomas Bailey, Peter Berg, and Arne Kalleberg, *Manufacturing Advantage: Why High-Performance Work Systems Pay Off* (ILR Press, 2000); Rosemary Batt and Eileen Appelbaum, "Worker Participation in Diverse Settings: Does the Form Affect the Outcome and If So, Who Benefits?" *British Journal of Industrial Relations* (September 1995): 353–378; Saul Rubinstein, Adrienne Eaton, and William Colucci, The Effects of High Performance Work Systems in the Pharmaceutical Industry on Employee Attitudes and Communications Networks (Rutgers University School of Management and Labor Relations, 2000).

36. Osterman, "Work Organization in an Era of Restructuring."

37. UNITE is a merged union. The partnership was originally formed by Xerox with the Amalgamated Clothing and Textile Workers Union. In 1995, ACTWU and the International Ladies Garment Workers Union merged to form UNITE.

38. See Joel Cutcher-Gershenfeld, Tracing a Transformation in Industrial Relations: The Case of the Xerox Corporation and the Amalgamated Clothing and Textile Workers Union (U.S. Department of Labor, 1988). For quantitative evidence of the effects of these innovations on performance at Xerox, see Cutcher-Gershenfeld, "The Impact on Economic Performance of a Transformation in Workplace Relations," *Industrial and Labor Relations Review* 44 (1991), January: 241–260.

39. Susan Eaton, Work-Family Integration in Biotechnology: Implications for Firms and Employees (Ph.D. dissertation, MIT Sloan School, 2000); Françoise Carré et al., Professional Pathways: Examining Work, Family and Community in the Biotechnology Industry (Report to Alfred P. Sloan Foundation, 1999).

Chapter 4

1. Daniel Yankelovich, national survey data from 1997 (on file with the authors).

2. See Collective Bargaining Forum, "Principles for New Employment Relationship," *Perspectives on Work* 3 (1999), no. 1: 22–29.

3. Much of our thinking on the need for unions to adopt an array of organizational forms was influenced by Task Force member Dorothy

Sue Cobble. For an excellent discussion of these themes, see Cobble, "Organizing the Postindustrial Work Force: Lessons from the History of Waitress Unionism," *Industrial and Labor Relations Review* 44 (1991): 419–437.

4. Thanks are due to Task Force member Amy Dean for coining this term.

5. Others have also proposed viewing unions as networks. See e.g, Charles Heckscher, *The New Unionism* (Basic Books, 1987); Saul Rubinstein and Charles Heckscher, "Labor Management Partnership: Two Views," in *Negotiations*, ed. T. Kochan and D. Lipsky (Cornell University Press, forthcoming).

6. Graham Staines and Robert Quinn, "American Workers Evaluate the Quality of Their Jobs," *Monthly Labor Review* 102 (1979), no. 1: 3–12.

7. See Thomas Kochan, Harry Katz, and Nancy Mower, "Worker Participation and American Unions," in *Challenges and Choices Facing American Labor*, ed. T. Kochan (MIT Press, 1985).

8. Seymour Lipset and Noah Meltz, "Canadian and American Attitudes Toward Work and Institutions," *Perspectives on Work* 1 (1998), no. 3: 14–19; Richard Freeman and Joel Rogers, *What Workers Want* (ILR Press, 1999); AFL-CIO, High Hopes, Little Trust: A Study of Young Workers and their Ups and Downs in the New Economy, 1999 (http: //www.aflcio.org/articles/high_hopes/index.htm).

9. Freeman and Rogers, *What Workers Want*, pp. 42–43.

10. Ibid., p. 52–53.

11. Peter D. Hart Research Associates, Inc., AFL-CIO Union Message survey (study 5433, March 29–31, 1999).

12. Morton Bahr, *From the Telegraph to the Internet* (National Press Books, 1998).

13. For a thorough review of the state of unionization and union man-agement relations over this period, see Harry Katz and Owen Darbashire, *Converging Divergences* (ILR Press, 1999).

14. Business Roundtable, Training Problems in Open Shop Construction (Construction Industry Cost Effectiveness Project, 1990) (www.brtable.org).

15. Home-care programs are not medical programs and are not home health services funded by Medicare or Medicaid.

16. Interview with Michael Gallagher, SEIU organizer of LA home-care workers, 1987–89, April 12, 1999.

17. Janice Fine, "Community Unionism: The Key to the New Labor Movement," *Perspectives on Work* 1 (1997), no. 2: 32–35.

18. Personal communication.

19. Elena Cabral, Building Safety Nets for the New York Work Force. Ford Foundation Report, spring-summer 1999, p. 5.

20. Thomas Kochan, Robert McKersie, and John Chalykoff, "The Effects of Corporate Strategy and Workplace Innovations on Union Representation," *Industrial and Labor Relations Review* 39 (1986), no. 4: 487–502.

21. High Road Partnerships Report: Innovations in Building Good Jobs and Strong Communities (AFL-CIO Working for America Institute, 2000).

22. Raymond Friedman and Donna Carter, African American Network Groups: Their Impact and Effectiveness (Executive Leadership Council, 1993).

23. Ibid. , p. 33.

Chapter 5

1. Jennifer Gordon, Latino Immigrants Change New York Wage Law: The Impact of Non-Voters on Politics and the Impact of Political Participation on Non-Voters (prepared for Ford Foundation, October 1998; presented at MIT Institute for Work and Employment Research, November 17, 1998).

2. Paul Osterman and Brenda Lautsch, Project QUEST; A Report to the Ford Foundation, 1997.

3. It also has spawned many for-profit organizations.

4. One such program replicated the California-based Centers for Employment and Training model for machining occupations. Another was a hotel training program inspired by the San Francisco program described in chapter 3 above.

5. Annette Bernhardt and Thomas Bailey, Making Careers Out of Jobs: Policies for a New Employment Relationship (mimeo, Institute on Education and the Economy, Teachers College, Columbia University, October 1997).

6. Erin Flynn and Robert Forrant, Facilitating Firm Level Change: The Role of Intermediary Organizations in the Manufacturing Modernization Process (Jobs for the Future, February 1995), p. 18.

7. David Autor, Outsourcing At Will: Unjust Dismissal Doctrine and the Growth of Temporary Help Employment (Working Paper 7557, National Bureau of Economic Research, 2000).

8. Staffing Industry Reports, January 12, 1997, p. 8.

9. Ibid., p. 11.

Chapter 6

1. Joel Cutcher-Gershenfeld, Thomas Kochan, and John Calhoun Wells, "How Do Labor and Management View Collective Bargaining?" *Monthly Labor Review* 121 (1998), no. 10: 23–31.

2. A program in Brazil seeks to attack the use of child labor while being sensitive to the root cause of why children are forced to work rather than go to school, namely they need to contribute to family income lest the family fall deeper into poverty. The experiment provides families with a grant equivalent to the minimum wage in return for ensuring their children attend school rather than work. Preliminary evaluations of this experiment show strong benefit/cost returns; see José Pastore, "Labor Standards and International Trade: The Case of Child Labor in Brazil," in Proceedings of Twelfth World Congress of the International Industrial Relations Association, Track 2 reports (2000).

3. Steven Greenhouse, "Banishing the Dickensian Factor," *New York Times*, July 9, 2000.

4. Lauri Bassi and Daniel McMurrer, "Coverage and Recipiency: Trends and Effects," in *Unemployment Insurance in the United States*, ed. C. O'Leary and S. Wandner (Upjohn Institute for Employment Research, 1997). These estimates are based on the SIPP survey and refer to the years 1989–1991.

5. Sanford Jacoby, *Employing Bureaucracy* (Columbia University Press, 1987); Daniel Nelson, *Managers and Workers: Origins of the New Factory System in the United States. 1880–1920* (University of Wisconsin Press, 1975).

6. Jacoby, *Modern Manors*.

7. Karen Ferguson and Kate Blackwell, *The Pension Book* (Arcade, 1995), p. 30.

8. Canadian jurisdictions have adopted this in a number of settings under the rubric of "internal-responsibility systems."

9. For discussions of a set of due process standards experts agree should be included in these dispute resolution processes, see Arnold Zack, "Bringing Fairness and Due Process to Employment Arbitration," *Negotiation Journal* 12 (1999), no. 2: 167–173; Richard Chaykowski, Joel Cutcher-Gershenfeld, Thomas Kochan, and Christina Sickles Merchant, *Facilitating Conflict Resolution in Union-Management Relations: A Guide for Neutrals* (Cornell/PERC Institute on Conflict Resolution, 1999).

10. For the results of the Massachusetts experiment, see Thomas Kochan, Brenda Lautsch, and Corinne Bendersky, "An Evaluation of the Massachusetts Commission Against Discrimination Alternative Dispute Resolution Program," *Harvard Negotiation Law Review* 5 (2000), spring: 233–278. See also E. Patrick McDermott, Ruth Obar, Anita Jose, and Mollie Bowers, An Evolution of the Equal Employment Opportunity Commission Mediation Program (www.eeoc.gov/mediate/report/index.html).

11. Commission on the Future of Worker-Management Relations (www.dol.gov/dol/_sec/public/media/reports/dunlop.summary.htm).

Chapter 7

1. See David Card and Alan Krueger, "Minimum Wages and Employment: A Case Study of the Fast-Food Industry in New Jersey and Pennsylvania," *American Economic Review* 84 (1994), no. 4, p. 772; David Neumark and William Wascher, "Employment Effects of Minimum and Subminimum Wages, Panel Data on State Minimum Wage Laws," *Industrial and Labor Relations Review* 46 (1992), no. 1: 55–81.

2. See Howard Wial, Minimum-Wage Enforcement and the Low-Wage Labor Market (Working Paper 11, MIT Task Force on Reconstructing America's Labor Market Institutions, 1999).

3. For evidence of the effects of unions in reducing intra-industry wage inequality, see Richard Freeman and James Medoff, *What Do Unions Do?* (Basic Books, 1984). For a multiple-plant, single-company study, see Anil Verma and Thomas Kochan, "Two Paths to Innovations in Industrial Relations: The Case of Canada and the United States," *Labor Law Journal* 41 (1990), no. 8: 601–607. For recent analyses using national samples of American and Canadian workers, see J. DiNardo, N. Fortin, and T. Lemieux, "Labor Market Institutions and the Distribution of Wages, 1973–1992: A Semi-Parametric Approach," *Econometrica* 64

(1996): 1001–1044; D. Card, F. Kramarz, and T. Lemieux, "Changes in the Relative Structure of Wages and Employment: A Comparison of the United States, Canada, and France," *Canadian Journal of Economics* 32 (1999): 843–877.

4. Eileen Appelbaum, personal communication.

5. See, e.g., George Shultz and Albert Rees, *Workers and Wages in an Urban Labor Market* (University of Chicago Press, 1970).

6. See James Rebitzer, "Industrial Relations Job Safety and Contract Workers in the Petrochemical Industry," *Industrial Relations* 34 (1995), no. 1: 40–57; Thomas Kochan, James Rebitzer, John Wells, and Michal Smith, "Human Resource Strategies and Contingent Workers: The Case of Safety and Health in the Petrochemical Industry," *Human Resource Management* 33 (1994), no. 1: 55–77.

7. Paul Osterman, "Work Organization in an Era of Restructuring: Trends in Diffusion and Impacts on Employee Welfare," *Industrial and Labor Relations Review* 53 (2000), no. 2: 179–196.

Index